MAD LIBS®

ALL I WANT FOR CHRISTMAS IS MAD LIBS

concept created by Roger Price and Leonard Stern

MAD LIBS

An Imprint of Penguin Random House LLC

Mad Libs format and text copyright © 1996, 2001, 2003, 2005, 2007, 2008, 2010, 2011, 2012, 2013
by Penguin Random House LLC. All rights reserved.

Concept created by Roger Price & Leonard Stern

All I Want for Christmas Is Mad Libs published in 2013 by Price Stern Sloan.
This edition published in 2017 by Mad Libs,
an imprint of Penguin Random House LLC, New York.
Printed in the USA.

Visit us online at penguinrandomhouse.com

All I Want For Christmas Is Mad Libs ISBN 9780843176667
9 10 8

MAD LIBS®

CHRISTMAS CAROL
MAD LIBS

concept created by Roger Price and Leonard Stern

Mad Libs
An Imprint of Penguin Random House

MAD LIBS

INSTRUCTIONS

MAD LIBS® is a game for people who don't like games!
It can be played by one, two, three, four, or forty.

• RIDICULOUSLY SIMPLE DIRECTIONS

In this tablet you will find stories containing blank spaces where words are left out. One player, the READER, selects one of these stories. The READER does not tell anyone what the story is about. Instead, he/she asks the other players, the WRITERS, to give him/her words. These words are used to fill in the blank spaces in the story.

• TO PLAY

The READER asks each WRITER in turn to call out a word—an adjective or a noun or whatever the space calls for—and uses them to fill in the blank spaces in the story. The result is a MAD LIBS® game.

When the READER then reads the completed MAD LIBS® game to the other players, they will discover that they have written a story that is fantastic, screamingly funny, shocking, silly, crazy, or just plain dumb—depending upon which words each WRITER called out.

• EXAMPLE (*Before and After*)

"_____!" he said _____
    EXCLAMATION   ADVERB

as he jumped into his convertible _____ and
                                          NOUN

drove off with his _____ wife.
                        ADJECTIVE

"*Ouch*_____!" he said *stupidly*_____
    EXCLAMATION   ADVERB

as he jumped into his convertible *cat*_____ and
                                          NOUN

drove off with his *brave*_____ wife.

QUICK REVIEW

In case you have forgotten what adjectives, adverbs, nouns, and verbs are, here is a quick review:

An ADJECTIVE describes something or somebody. *Lumpy, soft, ugly, messy,* and *short* are adjectives.

An ADVERB tells how something is done. It modifies a verb and usually ends in "ly." *Modestly, stupidly, greedily,* and *carefully* are adverbs.

A NOUN is the name of a person, place, or thing. *Sidewalk, umbrella, bridle, bathtub,* and *nose* are nouns.

A VERB is an action word. *Run, pitch, jump,* and *swim* are verbs. Put the verbs in past tense if the directions say PAST TENSE. *Ran, pitched, jumped,* and *swam* are verbs in the past tense.

When we ask for A PLACE, we mean any sort of place: a country or city *(Spain, Cleveland)* or a room *(bathroom, kitchen).*

An EXCLAMATION or SILLY WORD is any sort of funny sound, gasp, grunt, or outcry, like *Wow!, Ouch!, Whomp!, Ick!,* and *Gadzooks!*

When we ask for specific words, like a NUMBER, a COLOR, an ANIMAL, or a PART OF THE BODY, we mean a word that is one of those things, like *seven, blue, horse,* or *head.*

When we ask for a PLURAL, it means more than one. For example, *cat* pluralized is *cats.*

MAD LIBS® is fun to play with friends, but you can also play it by yourself! To begin with, DO NOT look at the story on the page below. Fill in the blanks on this page with the words called for. Then, using the words you have selected, fill in the blank spaces in the story.

Now you've created your own hilarious MAD LIBS® game!

JINGLE BELLS

PLURAL NOUN _____

ANIMAL _____

NOUN _____

PLURAL NOUN _____

VERB ENDING IN "ING" _____

PLURAL NOUN _____

PLURAL NOUN _____

VERB _____

PLURAL NOUN _____

SAME PLURAL NOUN _____

VERB _____

SAME ANIMAL _____

Dashing through the _____,
PLURAL NOUN

In a one-_____ open _____,
ANIMAL   NOUN

O'er the _____ we go,
PLURAL NOUN

_____ all the way.
VERB ENDING IN "ING"

_____ on bobtails ring,
PLURAL NOUN

Making _____ bright.
PLURAL NOUN

What fun it is to _____ and sing
VERB

A sleighing song tonight!

Jingle _____, jingle _____,
PLURAL NOUN   SAME PLURAL NOUN

Jingle all the way!

Oh, what fun it is to _____
VERB

In a one-_____ open sleigh.
SAME ANIMAL

GOING CAROLING

_____ ADJECTIVE

_____ ADJECTIVE

_____ NUMBER

_____ ADJECTIVE

_____ PLURAL NOUN

_____ PLURAL NOUN

_____ ADJECTIVE

_____ PLURAL NOUN

_____ NOUN

_____ PLURAL NOUN

_____ VERB

_____ NUMBER

_____ NOUN

_____ NUMBER

_____ ADVERB

_____ NOUN

_____ PLURAL NOUN

_____ VERB

MAD LIBS® is fun to play with friends, but you can also play it by yourself! To begin with, DO NOT look at the story on the page below. Fill in the blanks on this page with the words called for. Then, using the words you have selected, fill in the blank spaces in the story.

Now you've created your own hilarious MAD LIBS® game!

MAD LIBS®
GOING CAROLING

'Tis the _____ season for caroling! Here's how to make
　　　　　　ADJECTIVE

everyone's Christmas a little more merry and _____:
　　　　　　　　　　　　　　　　　　　　　　ADJECTIVE

- Gather _____ of your _____ friends and family
　　　　　　NUMBER　　　　　　　　ADJECTIVE

  _____ together. Pick out a few classic _____ to sing,
  PLURAL NOUN　　　　　　　　　　　　　　　PLURAL NOUN

  like "Have Yourself a/an _____ Little Christmas," "Silver
　　　　　　　　　　　　　ADJECTIVE

  _____," and "Frosty the _____-man."
  PLURAL NOUN　　　　　　　　　NOUN

- Put Santa _____ on everyone's heads and _____ to
　　　　　　PLURAL NOUN　　　　　　　　　　　　　　　VERB

  your neighbor's house.

- Knock _____ times on the front _____. Nothing? Knock
　　　　　NUMBER　　　　　　　　　　　　NOUN

  _____ more times _____.
  NUMBER　　　　　　　　ADVERB

- When your neighbor answers the _____, ask if he or she would
　　　　　　　　　　　　　　　　　　NOUN

  like to hear you sing a song. If your neighbor says yes, sing your

  _____ out. If your neighbor says no, _____ anyway!
  PLURAL NOUN　　　　　　　　　　　　　　　　VERB

MAD LIBS® is fun to play with friends, but you can also play it by yourself! To begin with, DO NOT look at the story on the page below. Fill in the blanks on this page with the words called for. Then, using the words you have selected, fill in the blank spaces in the story.

Now you've created your own hilarious MAD LIBS® game!

DECK THE HALLS

_____ PLURAL NOUN

_____ PLURAL NOUN

_____ NOUN

_____ ADJECTIVE

_____ ADJECTIVE

_____ ADJECTIVE

_____ VERB ENDING IN "ING"

_____ NOUN

_____ ADJECTIVE

_____ ADJECTIVE

MAD LIBS

DECK THE HALLS

Deck the _____ with boughs of _____,

PLURAL NOUN   PLURAL NOUN

Fa-la-la-la-la-la-la-la-la!

'Tis the _____ to be _____,

NOUN   ADJECTIVE

Fa-la-la-la-la-la-la-la-la!

Don we now our _____ apparel,

ADJECTIVE

Fa-la-la-la-la-la-la-la-la!

Troll the ancient _____ carol,

ADJECTIVE

Fa-la-la-la-la-la-la-la-la!

See the _____ Yule before us,

VERB ENDING IN "ING"

Fa-la-la-la-la-la-la-la-la!

Strike the _____ and join the chorus,

NOUN

Fa-la-la-la-la-la-la-la-la!

Follow me in _____ measure,

ADJECTIVE

Fa-la-la-la-la-la-la-la-la!

While I tell of _____ treasure,

ADJECTIVE

Fa-la-la-la-la-la-la-la-la!

THE TWELVE DAYS OF
CHRISTMAS, PART 1

NOUN _____

NOUN _____

NOUN _____

ADJECTIVE _____

NOUN _____

ADJECTIVE _____

ADJECTIVE _____

NOUN _____

PLURAL NOUN _____

ADJECTIVE _____

NOUN _____

MAD LIBS® is fun to play with friends, but you can also play it by yourself! To begin with, DO NOT look at the story on the page below. Fill in the blanks on this page with the words called for. Then, using the words you have selected, fill in the blank spaces in the story.

Now you've created your own hilarious MAD LIBS® game!

On the first day of Christmas,

My true _____ gave to me
NOUN

A partridge in a/an _____ tree.
NOUN

On the second _____ of Christmas,
NOUN

My _____ love gave to me
ADJECTIVE

Two turtle doves

And a/an _____ in a/an _____ tree.
NOUN   ADJECTIVE

On the third day of Christmas,

My _____ _____ gave to me
ADJECTIVE   NOUN

Three French hens,

Two turtle _____,
PLURAL NOUN

And a partridge in a/an _____ _____.
ADJECTIVE   NOUN

THE TWELVE DAYS OF CHRISTMAS, PART 2

_____ NOUN

_____ NUMBER

_____ ADJECTIVE

_____ NOUN

_____ ADJECTIVE

_____ NOUN

_____ PLURAL NOUN

_____ PLURAL NOUN

_____ ADJECTIVE

_____ PLURAL NOUN

_____ ADJECTIVE

_____ PLURAL NOUN

_____ NOUN

_____ ADJECTIVE

_____ NOUN

On the fourth day of Christmas,

My true _____ gave to me
<u>NOUN</u>

Four calling birds,

_____ French hens,
<u>NUMBER</u>

Two _____ doves,
<u>ADJECTIVE</u>

And a/an _____ in a pear tree.
<u>NOUN</u>

On the fifth day of Christmas,

My _____ _____ gave to me
<u>ADJECTIVE</u>   <u>NOUN</u>

Five golden _____,
<u>PLURAL NOUN</u>

Four calling _____,
<u>PLURAL NOUN</u>

Three _____ _____,
<u>ADJECTIVE</u>   <u>PLURAL NOUN</u>

Two _____ _____,
<u>ADJECTIVE</u>   <u>PLURAL NOUN</u>

And a/an _____ in a/an _____ _____.
<u>NOUN</u>   <u>ADJECTIVE</u>   <u>NOUN</u>

MAD LIBS® is fun to play with friends, but you can also play it by yourself! To begin with, DO NOT look at the story on the page below. Fill in the blanks on this page with the words called for. Then, using the words you have selected, fill in the blank spaces in the story.

Now you've created your own hilarious MAD LIBS® game!

CHRISTMAS SHOPPING

_____ ADJECTIVE

_____ ADJECTIVE

_____ PLURAL NOUN

_____ NOUN

_____ CELEBRITY

_____ VERB (PAST TENSE)

_____ VERB

_____ ADJECTIVE

_____ NOUN

_____ TYPE OF LIQUID

_____ ADJECTIVE

_____ ADJECTIVE

_____ NOUN

_____ PLURAL NOUN

_____ PLURAL NOUN

_____ PLURAL NOUN

_____ PLURAL NOUN

_____ NOUN

_____ VERB ENDING IN "ING"

MAD LIBS®
CHRISTMAS SHOPPING

When I was a/an _____ kid, I loved going to the
\qquad\qquad ADJECTIVE

_____ mall at Christmastime. My parents would dress me and
ADJECTIVE

my _____ in our cutest holiday outfits. Then we'd all pile into the
PLURAL NOUN

family _____ and drive to the mall to sit on _____'s
NOUN \qquad\qquad CELEBRITY

lap. As we _____ in the long line to Santa's _____-
VERB (PAST TENSE) \qquad VERB

shop, we'd look around at all the _____ lights strung around the
ADJECTIVE

_____, drink hot _____, and sing _____
NOUN \qquad TYPE OF LIQUID \qquad ADJECTIVE

carols. Then the _____ moment would arrive—we'd finally get
ADJECTIVE

to meet Santa and tell him what we wanted to find under the

_____ on Christmas morning. Of course, now that I'm older, I
NOUN

avoid the mall at all _____. It's so crowded that all the
PLURAL NOUN

_____ push into one another. You can't even catch of glimpse of
PLURAL NOUN

Santa and his _____. These days, I buy all my _____
PLURAL NOUN \qquad PLURAL NOUN

online. With just a click of the _____, Christmas _____
NOUN \qquad VERB ENDING IN "ING"

couldn't be easier!

THE CHRISTMAS PAGEANT

_____ ADJECTIVE

_____ A PLACE

_____ PLURAL NOUN

_____ PLURAL NOUN

_____ ADJECTIVE

_____ NOUN

_____ NOUN

_____ SILLY WORD

_____ PERSON IN ROOM (MALE)

_____ NOUN

_____ ADJECTIVE

_____ ADJECTIVE

_____ COLOR

_____ NOUN

_____ ADJECTIVE

_____ PART OF THE BODY (PLURAL)

_____ PLURAL NOUN

_____ SILLY WORD

MAD LIBS® is fun to play with friends, but you can also play it by yourself! To begin with, DO NOT look at the story on the page below. Fill in the blanks on this page with the words called for. Then, using the words you have selected, fill in the blank spaces in the story.

Now you've created your own hilarious MAD LIBS® game!

MAD LIBS

THE CHRISTMAS PAGEANT

Every December, our school puts on a/an _____ holiday
                                           ADJECTIVE

pageant. We decorate (the) _____ with snow _____
                              A PLACE   PLURAL NOUN

and red and green _____, and we perform a/an _____
                     PLURAL NOUN   ADJECTIVE

play and sing Christmas carols. This year, the _____ is set in the
                                                     NOUN

North Pole. Our music _____, Mrs. _____, cast my
                            NOUN   SILLY WORD

best friend, _____, as Santa. He will, of course, be wearing a
               PERSON IN ROOM (MALE)

red _____ stuffed with a/an _____ pillow so he'll look
       NOUN   ADJECTIVE

really _____. I was cast as Rudolph the _____-nosed
          ADJECTIVE   COLOR

_____. I'll be wearing _____ antlers on my
     NOUN   ADJECTIVE

_____. The rest of the class will be elves making
PART OF THE BODY (PLURAL)

_____ in Santa's workshop. I can't wait! Ho, _____,
 PLURAL NOUN   SILLY WORD

ho!

O CHRISTMAS TREE

_____ NOUN

_____ SAME NOUN

_____ ADJECTIVE

_____ SAME NOUN

_____ SAME NOUN

_____ ADJECTIVE

_____ ADJECTIVE

_____ PLURAL NOUN

_____ ADJECTIVE

_____ PLURAL NOUN

_____ SAME NOUN

_____ SAME NOUN

_____ ADJECTIVE

MAD LIBS® is fun to play with friends, but you can also play it by yourself! To begin with, DO NOT look at the story on the page below. Fill in the blanks on this page with the words called for. Then, using the words you have selected, fill in the blank spaces in the story.

Now you've created your own hilarious MAD LIBS® game!

O CHRISTMAS TREE

O Christmas _____, O Christmas _____,
        NOUN   SAME NOUN

How _____ are your branches!
        ADJECTIVE

O Christmas _____, O Christmas _____,
        SAME NOUN   SAME NOUN

How _____ are your branches!
        ADJECTIVE

They're _____ when summer _____ are bright,
            ADJECTIVE   PLURAL NOUN

They're _____ when winter _____ are white.
            ADJECTIVE   PLURAL NOUN

O Christmas _____, O Christmas _____,
        SAME NOUN   SAME NOUN

How _____ are your branches!
        ADJECTIVE

MAD LIBS® is fun to play with friends, but you can also play it by yourself! To begin with, DO NOT look at the story on the page below. Fill in the blanks on this page with the words called for. Then, using the words you have selected, fill in the blank spaces in the story.

Now you've created your own hilarious MAD LIBS® game!

UP ON THE HOUSETOP

_____ NOUN

_____ ANIMAL (PLURAL)

_____ ADJECTIVE

_____ NOUN

_____ ADJECTIVE

_____ PERSON IN ROOM

_____ PLURAL NOUN

_____ EXCLAMATION

_____ NOUN

_____ VERB

_____ PERSON IN ROOM

_____ NOUN

_____ SILLY WORD

_____ SAME SILLY WORD

_____ SAME SILLY WORD

_____ ADJECTIVE

MAD LIBS

UP ON THE HOUSETOP

Up on the _____-top, _____ pause,
             NOUN   ANIMAL (PLURAL)

Out jumps _____ old Santa Claus.
             ADJECTIVE

Down through the _____ with lots of toys,
                    NOUN

All for the _____ ones, Christmas joys.
               ADJECTIVE

Ho, ho, ho! Who wouldn't go? Ho, ho, ho! _____ wouldn't go!
                                          PERSON IN ROOM

First comes the _____ of little Nell.
                   PLURAL NOUN

_____! Dear Santa, fill it well!
   EXCLAMATION

Give her a/an _____ that laughs and cries,
                 NOUN

One that will _____ and shut its eyes.
                 VERB

Ho, ho, ho! Who wouldn't go? Ho, ho, ho! _____ wouldn't go!
                                          PERSON IN ROOM

Up on the _____-top, _____, _____,
             NOUN   SILLY WORD   SAME SILLY WORD

_____!
   SAME SILLY WORD

Down through the chimney with _____ Saint Nick.
                                 ADJECTIVE

A CHRISTMAS SOLO

_____ NOUN

_____ ADVERB

_____ ADJECTIVE

_____ VERB ENDING IN "ING"

_____ NUMBER

_____ NOUN

_____ VERB (PAST TENSE)

_____ COLOR

_____ PART OF THE BODY

_____ PERSON IN ROOM

_____ ADJECTIVE

_____ PLURAL NOUN

_____ ADJECTIVE

_____ PLURAL NOUN

_____ ADJECTIVE

_____ VERB (PAST TENSE)

_____ SAME VERB (PAST TENSE)

_____ NOUN

_____ ADJECTIVE

MAD LIBS®

A CHRISTMAS SOLO

A few years ago, my music _____ asked me to sing a Christmas
                              NOUN

solo at our holiday concert. At first I was _____ flattered, but the
                                            ADVERB

more I thought about it, the more _____ I became. Every time I
                                  ADJECTIVE

thought about _____ in front of _____ people, my
              VERB ENDING IN "ING"   NUMBER

whole _____ started to shake. What if I _____ or
      NOUN   VERB (PAST TENSE)

forgot the lyrics? What if I suddenly developed a/an _____ rash
                                                     COLOR

on my _____? My friend _____ suggested
       PART OF THE BODY   PERSON IN ROOM

picturing the audience as a bunch of _____ _____ to
                                     ADJECTIVE   PLURAL NOUN

make it easier. That seemed like a/an _____ plan—until I
                                      ADJECTIVE

worried I'd start laughing and all the _____ would think I was
                                       PLURAL NOUN

_____. Finally, the night of the concert arrived. I walked
ADJECTIVE

onstage, gathered all my courage, and _____ like I'd never
                                       VERB (PAST TENSE)

_____ before. The song went off without a/an
SAME VERB (PAST TENSE)

_____, and I received a standing ovation. It was the most
NOUN

_____ moment of my entire life!
ADJECTIVE

MAD LIBS® is fun to play with friends, but you can also play it by yourself! To begin with, DO NOT look at the story on the page below. Fill in the blanks on this page with the words called for. Then, using the words you have selected, fill in the blank spaces in the story.

Now you've created your own hilarious MAD LIBS® game!

AUNTIE'S CRAZY
CHRISTMAS CLOTHING

_____ PLURAL NOUN

_____ PLURAL NOUN

_____ ADJECTIVE

_____ PERSON IN ROOM (FEMALE)

_____ ADJECTIVE

_____ PLURAL NOUN

_____ PLURAL NOUN

_____ PART OF THE BODY

_____ PLURAL NOUN

_____ COLOR

_____ A PLACE

_____ NOUN

_____ PART OF THE BODY

_____ VERB (PAST TENSE)

_____ PART OF THE BODY

MAD LIBS
AUNTIE'S CRAZY
CHRISTMAS CLOTHING

Every Christmas, my family gets together to exchange _____ and
PLURAL NOUN

eat a big Christmas dinner of ham, mashed _____, and all the
PLURAL NOUN

_____ trimmings. For me, though, the highlight of every
ADJECTIVE

Christmas is seeing my aunt _____ make her
PERSON IN ROOM (FEMALE)

_____ entrance. She always wears the craziest _____
ADJECTIVE   PLURAL NOUN

on Christmas. You wouldn't believe it! For example, last year she wore

earrings that looked like giant Christmas _____, a sweatshirt with
PLURAL NOUN

Santa's _____ on the front, and socks with red-and-white
PART OF THE BODY

candy _____ on them. She also wore a snowflake pin with a
PLURAL NOUN

flashing _____ light that played "Santa Claus Is Coming to (the)
COLOR

_____," and she carried a/an _____ made out of
A PLACE   NOUN

tinsel. To top it all off, she tied bells to her _____ so she would
PART OF THE BODY

jingle when she _____! Gosh, that was almost as funny as the
VERB (PAST TENSE)

year she wrapped her entire _____ in Christmas lights! I can't
PART OF THE BODY

wait to see what she'll wear this year.

From CHRISTMAS CAROL MAD LIBS® • Copyright © 2003, 2007, 2012 by Penguin Random House LLC.

'TWAS THE NIGHT BEFORE
CHRISTMAS, PART 1

_____ NOUN

_____ ANIMAL

_____ PLURAL NOUN

_____ CELEBRITY (MALE)

_____ ADJECTIVE

_____ NUMBER

_____ ADJECTIVE

_____ ADJECTIVE

_____ SAME CELEBRITY

_____ PLURAL NOUN

_____ VERB (PAST TENSE)

_____ VERB (PAST TENSE)

_____ PERSON IN ROOM

_____ SILLY WORD

_____ SILLY WORD

_____ SILLY WORD

_____ NOUN

_____ VERB

_____ VERB

_____ VERB

MAD LIBS®
'TWAS THE NIGHT BEFORE CHRISTMAS, PART 1

'Twas the night before Christmas, when all through the _____,
NOUN

Not a creature was stirring, not even a/an _____.
ANIMAL

The _____ were hung by the chimney with care,
PLURAL NOUN

In hopes that _____ soon would be there.
CELEBRITY (MALE)

When, what to my wondering eyes should appear,

But a/an _____ sleigh and _____ _____
ADJECTIVE   NUMBER   ADJECTIVE

reindeer.

With a little old driver, so _____ and quick,
ADJECTIVE

I knew in a moment it must be _____.
SAME CELEBRITY

More rapid than _____, his reindeer they came,
PLURAL NOUN

As he _____ and _____ and called them by name:
VERB (PAST TENSE)   VERB (PAST TENSE)

"Now, _____! Now, Dancer! Now, _____ and Vixen!
PERSON IN ROOM   SILLY WORD

On, _____! On, Cupid! On, _____ and Blitzen!
SILLY WORD   SILLY WORD

To the top of the _____! To the top of the wall!
NOUN

Now _____ away! _____ away! _____
VERB   VERB   VERB

away, all!"

'TWAS THE NIGHT BEFORE CHRISTMAS, PART 2

_____ NOUN

_____ VERB ENDING IN "ING"

_____ VERB ENDING IN "ING"

_____ ADJECTIVE

_____ SAME CELEBRITY (FROM PART 1)

_____ PLURAL NOUN

_____ PLURAL NOUN

_____ VERB (PAST TENSE)

_____ PLURAL NOUN

_____ VERB (PAST TENSE)

_____ PART OF THE BODY

_____ NOUN

_____ VERB (PAST TENSE)

_____ ADJECTIVE

_____ ADJECTIVE

And then in a twinkling, I heard on the _____,

NOUN

The _____ and _____ of each

VERB ENDING IN "ING" — VERB ENDING IN "ING"

_____ hoof.

ADJECTIVE

And down the chimney _____ came, amid _____

SAME CELEBRITY (FROM PART I) — PLURAL NOUN

and soot.

He was covered in _____ from his head to his foot.

PLURAL NOUN

He _____ not a word, but went straight to his work,

VERB (PAST TENSE)

And filled all the _____, then _____ with

PLURAL NOUN — VERB (PAST TENSE)

a jerk.

And laying his _____ aside of his nose,

PART OF THE BODY

And giving a nod, up the _____ he rose!

NOUN

But I heard him exclaim as he _____ out of sight,

VERB (PAST TENSE)

"_____ Christmas to all, and to all a/an _____ night!"

ADJECTIVE — ADJECTIVE

MAD LIBS® is fun to play with friends, but you can also play it by yourself! To begin with, DO NOT look at the story on the page below. Fill in the blanks on this page with the words called for. Then, using the words you have selected, fill in the blank spaces in the story.

Now you've created your own hilarious MAD LIBS® game!

TOYLAND

_____ NOUN

_____ NOUN

_____ NOUN

_____ VERB

_____ ADJECTIVE

_____ NOUN

_____ ADJECTIVE

_____ ADJECTIVE

_____ PLURAL NOUN

Toyland, _____-land,
<u>NOUN</u>

Little _____ and _____ land,
<u>NOUN</u>   <u>NOUN</u>

While you _____ within it,
<u>VERB</u>

You are ever _____ there.
<u>ADJECTIVE</u>

_____'s joy land,
<u>NOUN</u>

_____, _____ Toyland!
<u>ADJECTIVE</u>   <u>ADJECTIVE</u>

Once you pass its _____,
<u>PLURAL NOUN</u>

You can never return again.

JOLLY OLD SAINT NICHOLAS

_____ ADJECTIVE

_____ PART OF THE BODY

_____ NOUN

_____ ADJECTIVE

_____ NUMBER

_____ NOUN

_____ ADVERB

_____ PLURAL NOUN

_____ VERB ENDING IN "ING"

_____ ADJECTIVE

_____ PLURAL NOUN

_____ NOUN

_____ ADJECTIVE

_____ VERB (PAST TENSE)

_____ ADJECTIVE

MAD☺LIBS®

JOLLY OLD SAINT NICHOLAS

Jolly _____ Saint Nicholas, lean your _____ this
      ADJECTIVE   PART OF THE BODY

way!

Don't you tell a single _____ what I'm going to say.
                     NOUN

Christmas Eve is coming soon; now you dear _____ man,
                             ADJECTIVE

Whisper what you'll bring to me; tell me if you can.

When the clock is striking _____, when I'm fast asleep,
                 NUMBER

Down the chimney with your _____, _____ you will creep.
                NOUN   ADVERB

All the _____ you will find, _____ in a row;
     PLURAL NOUN   VERB ENDING IN "ING"

Mine will be the _____ one—you'll be sure to know.
           ADJECTIVE

Johnny wants a pair of _____, Susie wants a/an _____,
         PLURAL NOUN   NOUN

Nellie wants a/an _____ book—one she hasn't _____.
        ADJECTIVE   VERB (PAST TENSE)

Now I think I'll leave to you what to give the rest.

Choose for me, _____ Santa Claus. You will know the best.
      ADJECTIVE

MAD LIBS® is fun to play with friends, but you can also play it by yourself! To begin with, DO NOT look at the story on the page below. Fill in the blanks on this page with the words called for. Then, using the words you have selected, fill in the blank spaces in the story.

Now you've created your own hilarious MAD LIBS® game!

OVER THE RIVER AND
THROUGH THE WOOD

_____ CELEBRITY

_____ NOUN

_____ NOUN

_____ ADJECTIVE

_____ ADJECTIVE

_____ NOUN

_____ NOUN

_____ VERB

_____ PART OF THE BODY (PLURAL)

_____ PART OF THE BODY

_____ NOUN

_____ NOUN

_____ NOUN

_____ PLURAL NOUN

_____ SILLY WORD

Over the river and through the wood,

To _____'s house we go.
       CELEBRITY

The _____ knows the way to carry the _____
       NOUN   NOUN

Through the _____ and _____ snow.
                ADJECTIVE   ADJECTIVE

Over the _____ and through the _____,
            NOUN   NOUN

Oh, how the wind does _____.
                            VERB

It stings the _____ and bites the _____
               PART OF THE BODY (PLURAL)   PART OF THE BODY

As over the _____ we go.
                NOUN

Over the river and through the _____,
                                    NOUN

To have a full _____ of play.
                   NOUN

Oh, hear the _____ ringing _____-a-ling-ling,
                PLURAL NOUN   SILLY WORD

For it is Christmas Day!

THE NAUGHTY LIST

ADJECTIVE
_____

NOUN
_____

ADJECTIVE
_____

ADVERB
_____

PLURAL NOUN
_____

NOUN
_____

PLURAL NOUN
_____

ADJECTIVE
_____

PLURAL NOUN
_____

NOUN
_____

PART OF THE BODY (PLURAL)
_____

NOUN
_____

NOUN
_____

ADJECTIVE
_____

SAME ADJECTIVE
_____

MAD LIBS® is fun to play with friends, but you can also play it by yourself! To begin with, DO NOT look at the story on the page below. Fill in the blanks on this page with the words called for. Then, using the words you have selected, fill in the blank spaces in the story.

Now you've created your own hilarious MAD LIBS® game!

MAD LIBS®
THE NAUGHTY LIST

Make sure you are always a/an _____ little girl or boy, or you
ADJECTIVE

might get a lump of coal in your _____ at Christmas! Here is a list
NOUN

of _____ things to do and *not* to do to stay off Santa's naughty
ADJECTIVE

list:

ALWAYS play _____ with your brothers and/or sisters and share
ADVERB

your _____ with them.
PLURAL NOUN

NEVER make a mess and then blame it on your pet _____.
NOUN

ALWAYS eat your green _____—even if they taste like
PLURAL NOUN

_____ _____.
ADJECTIVE PLURAL NOUN

ALWAYS make your _____ and brush your _____
NOUN PART OF THE BODY (PLURAL)

every morning.

NEVER tell your teacher that your _____ ate your homework—
NOUN

unless, of course, you can bring in a well-chewed _____ as proof.
NOUN

And always remember: Santa knows when you've been bad or

_____, so be _____, for goodness' sake!
ADJECTIVE SAME ADJECTIVE

FAVORITE
CHRISTMAS CAROLS

ADVERB _____

VERB ENDING IN "ING" _____

ADJECTIVE _____

ADJECTIVE _____

NOUN _____

CELEBRITY _____

COLOR _____

VERB _____

NOUN _____

NOUN _____

NOUN _____

COLOR _____

NOUN _____

MAD LIBS® is fun to play with friends, but you can also play it by yourself! To begin with, DO NOT look at the story on the page below. Fill in the blanks on this page with the words called for. Then, using the words you have selected, fill in the blank spaces in the story.

Now you've created your own hilarious MAD LIBS® game!

MAD LIBS
FAVORITE
CHRISTMAS CAROLS

Here's a list of the top ten most _____ played Christmas carols.
ADVERB

Which one is your favorite?

1) "The Christmas Song" ("Chestnuts _____ on a/an
VERB ENDING IN "ING"

_____ Fire")
ADJECTIVE

2) "Have Yourself a Merry _____ Christmas"
ADJECTIVE

3) "_____ Wonderland"
NOUN

4) "_____ Is Coming to Town"
CELEBRITY

5) "_____ Christmas"
COLOR

6) "Let It _____"
VERB

7) "Jingle _____ Rock"
NOUN

8) "Little Drummer _____"
NOUN

9) "_____ Ride"
NOUN

10) "Rudolph the _____-Nosed _____"
COLOR   NOUN

MAD LIBS® is fun to play with friends, but you can also play it by yourself! To begin with, DO NOT look at the story on the page below. Fill in the blanks on this page with the words called for. Then, using the words you have selected, fill in the blank spaces in the story.

Now you've created your own hilarious MAD LIBS® game!

WE WISH YOU A
MERRY CHRISTMAS

_____ ADJECTIVE

_____ SAME ADJECTIVE

_____ SAME ADJECTIVE

_____ ADJECTIVE

_____ ADJECTIVE

_____ PLURAL NOUN

_____ ADJECTIVE

_____ ADJECTIVE

_____ ADJECTIVE

_____ SAME ADJECTIVE

_____ SAME ADJECTIVE

_____ NOUN

_____ VERB

_____ SAME VERB

_____ SAME VERB

_____ VERB

We wish you a/an _____ Christmas,
ADJECTIVE

We wish you a/an _____ Christmas,
SAME ADJECTIVE

We wish you a/an _____ Christmas
SAME ADJECTIVE

And a/an _____ New Year.
ADJECTIVE

_____ tidings we bring
ADJECTIVE

To you and your _____,
PLURAL NOUN

_____ tidings for Christmas
ADJECTIVE

And a/an _____ New Year.
ADJECTIVE

Oh, bring us a/an _____ pudding,
ADJECTIVE

Oh, bring us a/an _____ pudding,
SAME ADJECTIVE

Oh, bring us a/an _____ pudding
SAME ADJECTIVE

And a cup of good _____.
NOUN

We won't _____ until we get some,
VERB

We won't _____ until we get some,
SAME VERB

We won't _____ until we get some,
SAME VERB

So _____ some out here.
VERB

A CHRISTMAS BLIZZARD

_____ ADJECTIVE

_____ ADJECTIVE

_____ PLURAL NOUN

_____ ADJECTIVE

_____ VERB ENDING IN "ING"

_____ ADJECTIVE

_____ NOUN

_____ NOUN

_____ NOUN

_____ NOUN

_____ NOUN

_____ NOUN

_____ ADJECTIVE

MAD LIBS® is fun to play with friends, but you can also play it by yourself! To begin with, DO NOT look at the story on the page below. Fill in the blanks on this page with the words called for. Then, using the words you have selected, fill in the blank spaces in the story.

Now you've created your own hilarious MAD LIBS® game!

MAD LIBS

A CHRISTMAS BLIZZARD

Have you been dreaming of a/an _____ Christmas? Me too! But
ADJECTIVE

what do you do when there is a/an _____ blizzard and you and
ADJECTIVE

your _____ get snowed in on Christmas? Here's a/an
PLURAL NOUN

_____ list of classic Christmas movies that'll keep
ADJECTIVE

everyone _____ for hours.
VERB ENDING IN "ING"

1) *It's a/an _____ Life*
ADJECTIVE

2) *Miracle on 34th _____*
NOUN

3) *A Christmas _____*
NOUN

4) *How the _____ Stole Christmas*
NOUN

5) *Frosty the Snow-_____*
NOUN

So just grab some pop-_____, throw a few more logs on the
NOUN

_____, and keep dreaming of a/an _____ white Christmas!
NOUN   ADJECTIVE

MAD LIBS® is fun to play with friends, but you can also play it by yourself! To begin with, DO NOT look at the story on the page below. Fill in the blanks on this page with the words called for. Then, using the words you have selected, fill in the blank spaces in the story.

Now you've created your own hilarious MAD LIBS® game!

HERE WE COME A-CAROLING

PLURAL NOUN _____

ADJECTIVE _____

VERB ENDING IN "ING" _____

ADJECTIVE _____

PLURAL NOUN _____

ADJECTIVE _____

ADJECTIVE _____

ADJECTIVE _____

NOUN _____

MAD LIBS
HERE WE COME A-CAROLING

Here we come a-caroling among the _____ so _____.
PLURAL NOUN   ADJECTIVE

Here we come a-_____ so _____ to be seen.
VERB ENDING IN "ING"   ADJECTIVE

Love and _____ come to you.
PLURAL NOUN

And to you _____ Christmas, too.
ADJECTIVE

And we wish you and send you a/an _____ New Year.
ADJECTIVE

And we wish you a/an _____ New _____.
ADJECTIVE   NOUN

MAD LIBS®

GRAB BAG
MAD LIBS

by Roger Price and Leonard Stern

INSTRUCTIONS

MAD LIBS® is a game for people who don't like games!
It can be played by one, two, three, four, or forty.

●RIDICULOUSLY SIMPLE DIRECTIONS

In this tablet you will find stories containing blank spaces where words are left out. One
player, the READER, selects one of these stories. The READER does not tell anyone
what the story is about. Instead, he/she asks the other players, the WRITERS, to give
him/her words. These words are used to fill in the blank spaces in the story.

●TO PLAY

The READER asks each WRITER in turn to call out a word—an adjective or a noun or
whatever the space calls for—and uses them to fill in the blank spaces in the story. The
result is a MAD LIBS® game.

When the READER then reads the completed MAD LIBS® game to the other players,
they will discover that they have written a story that is fantastic, screamingly funny,
shocking, silly, crazy, or just plain dumb—depending upon which words each WRITER
called out.

●EXAMPLE (*Before* and *After*)

"_____!" he said _____
         EXCLAMATION   ADVERB

as he jumped into his convertible _____ and
                                              NOUN

drove off with his _____ wife.
                         ADJECTIVE

"_____*Ouch*_____!" he said _____*stupidly*_____
         EXCLAMATION   ADVERB

as he jumped into his convertible _____*cat*_____ and
                                              NOUN

drove off with his _____*brave*_____ wife.
                         ADJECTIVE

QUICK REVIEW

In case you have forgotten what adjectives, adverbs, nouns, and verbs are, here is a quick review:

An ADJECTIVE describes something or somebody. *Lumpy, soft, ugly, messy,* and *short* are adjectives.

An ADVERB tells how something is done. It modifies a verb and usually ends in "ly." *Modestly, stupidly, greedily,* and *carefully* are adverbs.

A NOUN is the name of a person, place, or thing. *Sidewalk, umbrella, bridle, bathtub,* and *nose* are nouns.

A VERB is an action word. *Run, pitch, jump,* and *swim* are verbs. Put the verbs in past tense if the directions say PAST TENSE. *Ran, pitched, jumped,* and *swam* are verbs in the past tense.

When we ask for A PLACE, we mean any sort of place: a country or city *(Spain, Cleveland)* or a room *(bathroom, kitchen)*.

An EXCLAMATION or SILLY WORD is any sort of funny sound, gasp, grunt, or outcry, like *Wow!, Ouch!, Whomp!, Ick!,* and *Gadzooks!*

When we ask for specific words, like a NUMBER, a COLOR, an ANIMAL, or a PART OF THE BODY, we mean a word that is one of those things, like *seven, blue, horse,* or *head*.

When we ask for a PLURAL, it means more than one. For example, *cat* pluralized is *cats*.

MAD LIBS® is fun to play with friends, but you can also play it by yourself! To begin with, DO NOT look at the story on the page below. Fill in the blanks on this page with the words called for. Then, using the words you have selected, fill in the blank spaces in the story.

Now you've created your own hilarious MAD LIBS® game!

INTERVIEW WITH
A ROCK STAR

PLURAL NOUN _____

PLURAL NOUN _____

NOUN _____

COLOR _____

VERB _____

ADJECTIVE _____

NOUN _____

NOUN _____

ADJECTIVE _____

ADJECTIVE _____

NUMBER _____

ADJECTIVE _____

ADJECTIVE _____

ADJECTIVE _____

NOUN _____

VERB _____

MAD LIBS
INTERVIEW WITH
A ROCK STAR

QUESTION: Whatever made you choose the name "The Psycho

_____ " for your group?
   PLURAL NOUN

ANSWER: All the other good names like the "Rolling _____,"
                                           PLURAL NOUN

" _____ Jam," and " _____ Floyd" were taken.
   NOUN   COLOR

QUESTION: You not only _____ songs, but you play many
                             VERB

_____ instruments, don't you?
   ADJECTIVE

ANSWER: Yes. I play the electric _____, the bass _____,
                        NOUN   NOUN

and the _____ keyboard
    ADJECTIVE

QUESTION: You now have a/an _____ song that is number
                            ADJECTIVE

_____ on the _____ charts. What was the inspiration for
  NUMBER   ADJECTIVE

this _____ song?
   ADJECTIVE

ANSWER: Believe it or not, it was a/an _____ song that my
                               ADJECTIVE

mother used to sing to me when it was time for _____, and it
                                    NOUN

never failed to _____ me to sleep.
        VERB

HAVE I GOT
A GIRAFFE FOR YOU!

_____ PLURAL NOUN

_____ PLURAL NOUN

_____ PART OF THE BODY

_____ NUMBER

_____ PLURAL NOUN

_____ PART OF THE BODY

_____ TYPE OF LIQUID

_____ PART OF THE BODY (PLURAL)

_____ PART OF THE BODY

_____ ADJECTIVE

_____ PLURAL NOUN

_____ ADJECTIVE

_____ ADJECTIVE

_____ VERB ENDING IN "ING"

_____ NOUN

_____ PLURAL NOUN

_____ NOUN

MAD LIBS®
HAVE I GOT
A GIRAFFE FOR YOU!

Giraffes have aroused the curiosity of _____ since earliest times.
PLURAL NOUN

The giraffe is the tallest of all living _____, but scientists are
PLURAL NOUN

unable to explain how it got its long _____. The giraffe's
PART OF THE BODY

tremendous height, which might reach _____ _____,
NUMBER   PLURAL NOUN

comes mostly from its legs and _____. If a giraffe wants to
PART OF THE BODY

take a drink of _____ from the ground, it has to spread its
TYPE OF LIQUID

_____ far apart in order to reach down and lap up the
PART OF THE BODY (PLURAL)

water with its huge _____. The giraffe has _____
PART OF THE BODY   ADJECTIVE

ears that are sensitive to the faintest _____, and it has a/an
PLURAL NOUN

_____ sense of smell and sight. When attacked, a giraffe can put
ADJECTIVE

up a/an _____ fight by _____ out with its hind
ADJECTIVE   VERB ENDING IN "ING"

legs and using its head like a sledge _____. Finally, a giraffe can
NOUN

gallop at more than thirty _____ an hour when pursued and can
PLURAL NOUN

outrun the fastest _____.
NOUN

THE OLYMPICS

_____ NOUN

_____ PLURAL NOUN

_____ ADJECTIVE

_____ PLURAL NOUN

_____ PLURAL NOUN

_____ NUMBER

_____ ADJECTIVE

_____ ADJECTIVE

_____ NOUN

_____ ADJECTIVE

_____ VERB ENDING IN "S"

_____ PART OF THE BODY

_____ NOUN

_____ ADJECTIVE

_____ PLURAL NOUN

_____ PLURAL NOUN

MAD LIBS
THE OLYMPICS

Every four years, countries from all over the _____ send their best

<u>NOUN</u>

_____ to compete in _____ games and win _____.

<u>PLURAL NOUN</u>   <u>ADJECTIVE</u>   <u>PLURAL NOUN</u>

These events are called the Olympic _____, and they started

<u>PLURAL NOUN</u>

_____ years ago in _____ Greece. When a winner

<u>NUMBER</u>   <u>ADJECTIVE</u>

receives his or her _____ medal at the games, the national

<u>ADJECTIVE</u>

_____ of his or her country is played by a/an _____

<u>NOUN</u>   <u>ADJECTIVE</u>

band. As the band _____, the citizens of that country put

<u>VERB ENDING IN "S"</u>

their _____ to their chest and join in the singing of their

<u>PART OF THE BODY</u>

national _____. Thanks to television, these _____ events

<u>NOUN</u>   <u>ADJECTIVE</u>

can now be watched by over a billion _____ throughout the world

<u>PLURAL NOUN</u>

every four _____.

<u>PLURAL NOUN</u>

HOME SWEET HOME

NOUN _____

PART OF THE BODY _____

NUMBER _____

NOUN _____

COLOR _____

ADJECTIVE _____

NOUN _____

NOUN _____

PLURAL NOUN _____

NOUN _____

NOUN _____

ADJECTIVE _____

NOUN _____

ADVERB _____

PART OF THE BODY _____

VERB ENDING IN "ING" _____

ADJECTIVE _____

MAD LIBS® is fun to play with friends, but you can also play it by yourself! To begin with, DO NOT look at the story on the page below. Fill in the blanks on this page with the words called for. Then, using the words you have selected, fill in the blank spaces in the story.

Now you've created your own hilarious MAD LIBS® game!

MAD LIBS
HOME SWEET HOME

Some people are fond of the saying, "Home is where you hang your

_____." Others say, "Home is where the _____
    NOUN   PART OF THE BODY

is." As for me, even though my home is a rustic, _____-story
                                                NUMBER

_____ home with a/an _____ picket fence surrounding
    NOUN   COLOR

it, I think of it as my _____ castle. Perched on a/an
                            ADJECTIVE

_____ overlooking a babbling _____ and surrounded by
    NOUN   NOUN

a forest of huge _____, my home offers me _____ and
                PLURAL NOUN   NOUN

tranquility. Each and every _____ I look forward to coming back
                            NOUN

to my _____ home, where my faithful _____ will
          ADJECTIVE   NOUN

_____ greet me by wagging its _____ and
    ADVERB   PART OF THE BODY

_____ all over me. I just love my home _____ home.
VERB ENDING IN "ING"   ADJECTIVE

MAD LIBS® is fun to play with friends, but you can also play it by yourself! To begin with, DO NOT look at the story on the page below. Fill in the blanks on this page with the words called for. Then, using the words you have selected, fill in the blank spaces in the story.

Now you've created your own hilarious MAD LIBS® game!

INTERVIEW WITH A COMEDIAN

_____ NOUN

_____ ADJECTIVE

_____ ADJECTIVE

_____ NOUN

_____ NUMBER

_____ PLURAL NOUN

_____ NOUN

_____ VERB

_____ VERB

_____ PLURAL NOUN

_____ PLURAL NOUN

_____ ADJECTIVE

_____ NOUN

MAD LIBS
INTERVIEW WITH A COMEDIAN

QUESTION: Were you always a stand-up _____ ?

NOUN

ANSWER: No. I had many _____ jobs in my _____

ADJECTIVE ADJECTIVE

lifetime. I started out as a used _____ salesperson, and then for

NOUN

_____ years, I sold ladies' _____ .

NUMBER PLURAL NOUN

QUESTION: When did you discover you were a funny _____

NOUN

who could make people _____ out loud?

VERB

ANSWER: It was in school. The first time our teacher had us do show and

_____ , I made the _____ in my class laugh so hard

VERB PLURAL NOUN

they fell out of their _____ .

PLURAL NOUN

QUESTION: How would you describe your _____ act?

ADJECTIVE

ANSWER: I am a thinking person's _____ .

NOUN

MAD LIBS® is fun to play with friends, but you can also play it by yourself! To begin with, DO NOT look at the story on the page below. Fill in the blanks on this page with the words called for. Then, using the words you have selected, fill in the blank spaces in the story.

Now you've created your own hilarious MAD LIBS® game!

MOVIES SHOULD BE FUN

_____ PLURAL NOUN

_____ ADJECTIVE

_____ PLURAL NOUN

_____ NOUN

_____ ADJECTIVE

_____ NOUN

_____ NOUN

_____ PERSON IN ROOM (MALE)

_____ A PLACE

_____ ADJECTIVE

_____ PERSON IN ROOM

_____ PERSON IN ROOM

_____ ADJECTIVE

_____ PLURAL NOUN

_____ PART OF THE BODY (PLURAL)

MAD LIBS
MOVIES SHOULD BE FUN

In recent years, there have been too many disaster movies in which tall

_____ catch on fire, _____ dinosaurs come to life, and
 PLURAL NOUN   ADJECTIVE

huge _____ attack people in the ocean, making you afraid to get
      PLURAL NOUN

out of your _____ in the morning. Movie fans ask why we can't
            NOUN

have more _____ pictures like *It's a Wonderful* _____,
          ADJECTIVE   NOUN

Gone with the _____, or *Mr.* _____ *Goes to (the)*
               NOUN   PERSON IN ROOM (MALE)

_____. These films made you feel _____ all over.
 A PLACE   ADJECTIVE

These same fans also ask why we can't have more funny films with comedians

such as Laurel and _____, and Abbott and _____.
                  PERSON IN ROOM   PERSON IN ROOM

These _____ performers gave us great slapstick _____
       ADJECTIVE   PLURAL NOUN

that still makes our _____ ache from laughing.
                    PART OF THE BODY (PLURAL)

MAD LIBS® is fun to play with friends, but you can also play it by yourself! To begin with, DO NOT look at the story on the page below. Fill in the blanks on this page with the words called for. Then, using the words you have selected, fill in the blank spaces in the story.

Now you've created your own hilarious MAD LIBS® game!

COOL IT

PLURAL NOUN _____

ADJECTIVE _____

NOUN _____

ADJECTIVE _____

NOUN _____

NOUN _____

NOUN _____

NOUN _____

ADJECTIVE _____

VERB ENDING IN "ING" _____

NOUN _____

ADJECTIVE _____

NOUN _____

VERB _____

MAD LIBS
COOL IT

Weather plays an important part in our daily _____. What is
                                              PLURAL NOUN

weather anyway? According to _____ scientists, who are known
                               ADJECTIVE

as meteorologists, weather is what the air is like at any time of the

_____. It doesn't matter if the air is cold, hot, or _____,
        NOUN   ADJECTIVE

it's all weather. Weather changes from hour to _____, from day to
                                                    NOUN

_____, from season to _____, and from year to
      NOUN   NOUN

_____. Daily changes in weather are caused by _____
      NOUN   ADJECTIVE

storms _____ across the earth. Seasonal changes are from the
        VERB ENDING IN "ING"

earth moving around the _____. When the vapors in _____
                              NOUN   ADJECTIVE

clouds condense, we have _____ and snow. Whether you like it or
                              NOUN

not, weather is here to _____.
                              VERB

GOING TO TOWN

_____
LAST NAME

_____
ADJECTIVE

_____
PLURAL NOUN

_____
ADJECTIVE

_____
PERSON IN ROOM

_____
PLURAL NOUN

_____
PLURAL NOUN

_____
ADJECTIVE

_____
NOUN

_____
NUMBER

_____
VERB ENDING IN "ING"

_____
ADJECTIVE

_____
ADJECTIVE

_____
ADJECTIVE

_____
NOUN

_____
NOUN

MAD LIBS® is fun to play with friends, but you can also play it by yourself! To begin with, DO NOT look at the story on the page below. Fill in the blanks on this page with the words called for. Then, using the words you have selected, fill in the blank spaces in the story.

Now you've created your own hilarious MAD LIBS® game!

MAD LIBS

GOING TO TOWN

THE ART SCENE

Today the _____ Gallery presents a series of _____
      LAST NAME   ADJECTIVE

landscape paintings and still-life _____ by the _____
                PLURAL NOUN   ADJECTIVE

artist, _____. These beautiful _____ will be on
      PERSON IN ROOM   PLURAL NOUN

exhibition for the next three _____.
                  PLURAL NOUN

MUSIC

Tonight marks the _____ debut of the all- _____ choir
          ADJECTIVE   NOUN

of _____ great _____ voices. This _____
  NUMBER   VERB ENDING IN "ING"   ADJECTIVE

ensemble will present _____ renditions of such _____
           ADJECTIVE   ADJECTIVE

children's songs as "Twinkle Twinkle Little _____" and "Old
                          NOUN

MacDonald Had a/an _____."
          NOUN

THE THREE MUSKETEERS

ADJECTIVE _____

PLURAL NOUN _____

ADJECTIVE _____

NOUN _____

ADJECTIVE _____

NOUN _____

NOUN _____

PLURAL NOUN _____

NOUN _____

PERSON IN ROOM _____

PLURAL NOUN _____

ADJECTIVE _____

NOUN _____

NOUN _____

PLURAL NOUN _____

NOUN _____

MAD LIBS® is fun to play with friends, but you can also play it by yourself! To begin with, DO NOT look at the story on the page below. Fill in the blanks on this page with the words called for. Then, using the words you have selected, fill in the blank spaces in the story.

Now you've created your own hilarious MAD LIBS® game!

MAD LIBS

THE THREE MUSKETEERS

There is no more rousing story in _____ literature than *The*
                                   ADJECTIVE

Three _____. This _____ romance by the great French
          PLURAL NOUN   ADJECTIVE

_____, Alexander Dumas, tells the story of D' Artagnan, a/an
   NOUN

_____ young _____ who arrives in 17th-century Paris
    ADJECTIVE   NOUN

riding a/an _____ with only three _____ in his pocket.
               NOUN   PLURAL NOUN

Determined to be in the service of the _____ who rules all of
                                            NOUN

France, he duels with Athos, Pathos, and _____, three of the
                                          PERSON IN ROOM

king's best _____. Eventually, these swordsmen and D' Artagnan
              PLURAL NOUN

save their _____ king from being overthrown and losing his
              ADJECTIVE

_____. Over the years, *The Three Musketeers* has been made into a
   NOUN

stage _____, two motion _____, and, most recently,
         NOUN   PLURAL NOUN

into a Broadway _____.
                     NOUN

SNOW WHITE

PLURAL NOUN _____

PLURAL NOUN _____

ADJECTIVE _____

PLURAL NOUN _____

ADJECTIVE _____

NOUN _____

NOUN _____

ADJECTIVE _____

ADJECTIVE _____

PLURAL NOUN _____

NOUN _____

COLOR _____

NOUN _____

PART OF THE BODY _____

ADVERB _____

MAD LIBS® is fun to play with friends, but you can also play it by yourself! To begin with, DO NOT look at the story on the page below. Fill in the blanks on this page with the words called for. Then, using the words you have selected, fill in the blank spaces in the story.

Now you've created your own hilarious MAD LIBS® game!

MAD LIBS
SNOW WHITE

One of the most popular fairy _____ of all time is *Snow White*
PLURAL NOUN

and the Seven _____. Snow White is a princess whose _____
PLURAL NOUN   ADJECTIVE

beauty threatens her stepmother, the queen, and her two step-_____,
PLURAL NOUN

who are very _____. Snow White is forced to flee from the
ADJECTIVE

_____ in which she lives and hide in the nearby _____.
NOUN   NOUN

Once there, she is discovered by _____ animals who guide her to
ADJECTIVE

the _____ cottage of the seven dwarfs. The dwarfs come home
ADJECTIVE

from digging in their mine and discover Snow White asleep in their

_____. The dwarfs take care of her until a prince, who has traveled
PLURAL NOUN

the four corners of the _____ in search of Snow _____,
NOUN   COLOR

arrives and gives her a magical _____ on her _____,
NOUN   PART OF THE BODY

which miraculously brings her back to life. Snow White and the prince live

_____ ever after.
ADVERB

MAGIC, ANYONE?

PLURAL NOUN _____

ADJECTIVE _____

ADJECTIVE _____

NOUN _____

NOUN _____

NOUN _____

NOUN _____

ADJECTIVE _____

PART OF THE BODY _____

PLURAL NOUN _____

ADJECTIVE _____

NOUN _____

ADJECTIVE _____

NOUN _____

PART OF THE BODY (PLURAL) _____

PART OF THE BODY _____

PLURAL NOUN _____

MAD LIBS® is fun to play with friends, but you can also play it by yourself! To begin with, DO NOT look at the story on the page below. Fill in the blanks on this page with the words called for. Then, using the words you have selected, fill in the blank spaces in the story.

Now you've created your own hilarious MAD LIBS® game!

MAD LIBS®
MAGIC, ANYONE?

_____ of all ages enjoy watching _____ magicians
  PLURAL NOUN   ADJECTIVE

perform their _____ tricks. Every man, woman, and _____
                ADJECTIVE   NOUN

loves to see a magician pull a/an _____ out of a hat, saw a live
                                    NOUN

_____ in half, or make a huge _____ disappear into
   NOUN   NOUN

_____ air. Audiences love when magicians perform sleight of
  ADJECTIVE

_____ with a deck of _____, a/an _____
PART OF THE BODY   PLURAL NOUN   ADJECTIVE

coin, or a silk _____. The greatest of all magicians was the
                  NOUN

_____ Harry Houdini, who was able to escape from a locked
  ADJECTIVE

_____ even though his _____ were tied
   NOUN   PART OF THE BODY (PLURAL)

behind his _____ and his feet were wrapped in iron _____.
            PART OF THE BODY   PLURAL NOUN

THE BIG GAME

_____ PLURAL NOUN

_____ PERSON IN ROOM

_____ NOUN

_____ LAST NAME

_____ PLURAL NOUN

_____ A PLACE

_____ PLURAL NOUN

_____ A PLACE

_____ PLURAL NOUN

_____ NOUN

_____ ADJECTIVE

_____ ADJECTIVE

_____ NOUN

_____ NOUN

_____ NOUN

_____ VERB

_____ ADJECTIVE

MAD LIBS® is fun to play with friends, but you can also play it by yourself! To begin with, DO NOT look at the story on the page below. Fill in the blanks on this page with the words called for. Then, using the words you have selected, fill in the blank spaces in the story.

Now you've created your own hilarious MAD LIBS® game!

MAD LIBS
THE BIG GAME

To be read with great enthusiasm!

Hello there, sports _____! This is _____, talking to
                        PLURAL NOUN   PERSON IN ROOM

you from the press _____ in _____ Stadium, where
                        NOUN   LAST NAME

57,000 cheering _____ have gathered to watch (the) _____
                   PLURAL NOUN   A PLACE

_____ take on (the) _____ _____. Even
  PLURAL NOUN   A PLACE   PLURAL NOUN

though the _____ is shining, it's a/an _____ cold day
               NOUN   ADJECTIVE

with the temperature in the _____ 20s. A strong _____
                                ADJECTIVE   NOUN

is blowing fiercely across the playing _____ that will definitely
                                           NOUN

affect the passing _____. We'll be back for the opening
                        NOUN

_____ -off after a few words from our _____ sponsor.
     VERB   ADJECTIVE

THINGS TO DO
THIS WEEKEND

LAST NAME _____

ADJECTIVE _____

PLURAL NOUN _____

PLURAL NOUN _____

NOUN _____

ADJECTIVE _____

NOUN _____

ADVERB _____

NOUN _____

ADJECTIVE _____

PLURAL NOUN _____

PERSON IN ROOM _____

ADJECTIVE _____

NOUN _____

ADJECTIVE _____

ADJECTIVE _____

NOUN _____

NOUN _____

ADJECTIVE _____

FILM

_____ Theaters offers a/an _____ program of foreign
    LAST NAME   ADJECTIVE

_____ never before seen in American _____. The first
    PLURAL NOUN   PLURAL NOUN

film to be shown will be *Henry and the* _____. This is the
                                                   NOUN

_____ love story of a man and his _____. It will be
    ADJECTIVE   NOUN

shown _____ until the end of the _____.
        ADVERB   NOUN

STAGE

Appearing in our _____ theater for the next three _____
                 ADJECTIVE   PLURAL NOUN

is _____, that very _____ star of stage, screen, and
    PERSON IN ROOM   ADJECTIVE

_____. He/she will be appearing with our _____
    NOUN   ADJECTIVE

repertory company in nightly performances of William Shakespeare's

_____ comedy, *A Midsummer Night's* _____. Tickets
    ADJECTIVE   NOUN

can be purchased now at the _____ office by telephone, fax, or
                                  NOUN

_____ card.
    ADJECTIVE

SCENE FROM A HORROR PICTURE

NOUN _____

NOUN _____

ADVERB _____

VERB _____

ADJECTIVE _____

PART OF THE BODY _____

NOUN _____

PERSON IN ROOM _____

PART OF THE BODY _____

NOUN _____

EXCLAMATION _____

PLURAL NOUN _____

ADJECTIVE _____

NOUN _____

PLURAL NOUN _____

PART OF THE BODY _____

ADJECTIVE _____

MAD LIBS® is fun to play with friends, but you can also play it by yourself! To begin with, DO NOT look at the story on the page below. Fill in the blanks on this page with the words called for. Then, using the words you have selected, fill in the blank spaces in the story.

Now you've created your own hilarious MAD LIBS® game!

MAD LIBS
SCENE FROM A
HORROR PICTURE

To be read aloud (preferably by live people):

Actor #1: Why did we have to come to this _____ old castle?
ADJECTIVE

This place sends shivers up and down my _____.
PART OF THE BODY

Actor #2: We had no choice. You know all the _____ in town were
PLURAL NOUN

filled because of the _____ convention.
NOUN

Actor #1: I'd have been happy to stay in a/an _____ motel.
ADJECTIVE

Actor #2: Relax. Here comes the bellboy for our _____.
PLURAL NOUN

Actor #1: _____! Look, he's all bent over and has a big
EXCLAMATION

_____ riding on his _____. He looks just like
NOUN   PART OF THE BODY

_____ from that horror flick, *Frankenstein*.
PERSON IN ROOM

Actor #2: No. I think he's my old _____ teacher.
NOUN

Actor #1: I'm putting my _____ down! I'm not staying in this
PART OF THE BODY

_____ place. I'd rather _____ in the car!
ADJECTIVE   VERB

Actor #2: You're worrying _____.
ADVERB

Actor #1: Really? Look at the bellboy. He has my _____ in one
NOUN

hand, your _____ in the other, and his third hand . . . His *third*
NOUN

hand? Ahhhhh!

From GRAB BAG MAD LIBS® • Copyright © 1996, 2001, 2012 by Penguin Random House LLC.

MAD LIBS® is fun to play with friends, but you can also play it by yourself! To begin with, DO NOT look at the story on the page below. Fill in the blanks on this page with the words called for. Then, using the words you have selected, fill in the blank spaces in the story.

Now you've created your own hilarious MAD LIBS® game!

IN THE GOOD OLD SUMMERTIME

PLURAL NOUN _____

PLURAL NOUN _____

ADVERB _____

VERB ENDING IN "ING" _____

ADJECTIVE _____

NUMBER _____

PART OF THE BODY _____

PLURAL NOUN _____

NOUN _____

PLURAL NOUN _____

TYPE OF LIQUID _____

NOUN _____

ADVERB _____

PLURAL NOUN _____

PLURAL NOUN _____

NOUN _____

NOUN _____

NOUN _____

NOUN _____

Many selective _____ prefer the Summer Olympics to the Winter
_{PLURAL NOUN}

_____. They respond _____ to such swimming and
_{PLURAL NOUN}   _{ADVERB}

_____ competitions as the hundred-meter _____
_{VERB ENDING IN "ING"}   _{ADJECTIVE}

-style race, the _____-meter _____-stroke race, and, of
_{NUMBER}   _{PART OF THE BODY}

course, the diving contests in which _____ dive off a high
_{PLURAL NOUN}

_____ and do triple _____ in the air before landing in
_{NOUN}   _{PLURAL NOUN}

the _____. Equally fascinating are the track and _____
_{TYPE OF LIQUID}   _{NOUN}

events in which _____ conditioned _____ compete for
_{ADVERB}   _{PLURAL NOUN}

gold _____. They compete in such exciting events as the 1,500-
_{PLURAL NOUN}

_____ race, the hundred- _____ dash, the ever-popular
_{NOUN}   _{NOUN}

_____ vaulting, and, last but not least, throwing the hammer, the
_{NOUN}

javelin, and the _____.
_{NOUN}

MAD LIBS® is fun to play with friends, but you can also play it by yourself! To begin with, DO NOT look at the story on the page below. Fill in the blanks on this page with the words called for. Then, using the words you have selected, fill in the blank spaces in the story.

Now you've created your own hilarious MAD LIBS® game!

GOOD MANNERS

NOUN _____

NOUN _____

NOUN _____

VERB _____

PART OF THE BODY _____

ADVERB _____

NOUN _____

NOUN _____

NOUN _____

PART OF THE BODY (PLURAL) _____

NOUN _____

ADJECTIVE _____

ADVERB _____

1. When you receive a birthday _____ or a wedding _____,
NOUN   NOUN

you should always send a thank-you _____.
                                  NOUN

2. When you _____ or burp out loud, be sure to cover your
          VERB

_____ and say, "I'm _____ sorry."
PART OF THE BODY   ADVERB

3. If you are a man and wearing a/an _____ on your head and a/an
                            NOUN

_____ approaches, it's always polite to tip your _____.
NOUN   NOUN

4. When you are at a friend's _____ for dinner, remember, it's not
                        NOUN

polite to eat with your _____, take food from
                    PART OF THE BODY (PLURAL)

anyone else's _____, or leave the table before everyone else.
              NOUN

5. When meeting your friend's parents, always try to make a/an _____
                                                 ADJECTIVE

impression by greeting them _____.
                             ADVERB

TV GUIDANCE
PICK OF THE WEEK

_____ NOUN

_____ ADJECTIVE

_____ NUMBER

_____ PLURAL NOUN

_____ PLURAL NOUN

_____ NOUN

_____ PART OF THE BODY (PLURAL)

_____ ADJECTIVE

_____ PERSON IN ROOM (FEMALE)

_____ NOUN

_____ PART OF THE BODY

_____ PLURAL NOUN

_____ ADJECTIVE

_____ ADJECTIVE

_____ PERSON IN ROOM

_____ NOUN

_____ NOUN

MAD LIBS® is fun to play with friends, but you can also play it by yourself! To begin with, DO NOT look at the story on the page below. Fill in the blanks on this page with the words called for. Then, using the words you have selected, fill in the blank spaces in the story.

Now you've created your own hilarious MAD LIBS® game!

MAD LIBS
TV GUIDANCE
PICK OF THE WEEK

THURSDAY, 8:00 P.M. *My Adventures as a Foreign* _____.

NOUN

This is an exciting and _____ made-for-TV movie that takes

ADJECTIVE

place during the time of World War _____. We give it a rating of

NUMBER

three _____.

PLURAL NOUN

FRIDAY, 7:30 P.M. *Happy* _____.

PLURAL NOUN

When an old high-school _____ welcomes him with open

NOUN

_____ and throws him a/an _____ party, this

PART OF THE BODY (PLURAL) — ADJECTIVE

puts _____, his former _____ friend, into a bad

PERSON IN ROOM (FEMALE) — NOUN

state of _____.

PART OF THE BODY

SATURDAY, 10:00 P.M. *Where Have All the* _____ *Gone?* This

PLURAL NOUN

_____ thriller, by the _____ director

ADJECTIVE — ADJECTIVE

_____, is about a Manhattan _____ searching for a

PERSON IN ROOM — NOUN

missing person in a small _____.

NOUN

MAD LIBS® is fun to play with friends, but you can also play it by yourself! To begin with, DO NOT look at the story on the page below. Fill in the blanks on this page with the words called for. Then, using the words you have selected, fill in the blank spaces in the story.

Now you've created your own hilarious MAD LIBS® game!

GOOD HEALTH
TO ONE AND ALL

_____ ADJECTIVE

_____ ADJECTIVE

_____ VERB ENDING IN "ING"

_____ PART OF THE BODY (PLURAL)

_____ PLURAL NOUN

_____ PLURAL NOUN

_____ NOUN

_____ PLURAL NOUN

_____ PLURAL NOUN

_____ NOUN

_____ PLURAL NOUN

_____ PLURAL NOUN

_____ ADJECTIVE

_____ PLURAL NOUN

_____ ADJECTIVE

_____ ADJECTIVE

MAD LIBS
GOOD HEALTH
TO ONE AND ALL

A/An _____ fitness revolution is taking place. Today, millions of
       ADJECTIVE

people are doing all kinds of _____ exercises such as jogging,
           ADJECTIVE

walking, and _____ to get their _____
      VERB ENDING IN "ING"   PART OF THE BODY (PLURAL)

in shape and develop their _____. Many go to gyms and health
           PLURAL NOUN

_____ to work out by punching a/an _____, lifting
 PLURAL NOUN   NOUN

_____, or performing aerobic _____. In the past
 PLURAL NOUN   PLURAL NOUN

_____ people have become very weight conscious. They have
   NOUN

learned what _____ they should and should not eat. They know it's
       PLURAL NOUN

healthy to eat green _____ and _____ fruit. They also
        PLURAL NOUN   ADJECTIVE

know to avoid foods high in _____ and _____ fats,
          PLURAL NOUN   ADJECTIVE

especially if they want to lead a long and _____ life.
                  ADJECTIVE

MAD LIBS® is fun to play with friends, but you can also play it by yourself! To begin with, DO NOT look at the story on the page below. Fill in the blanks on this page with the words called for. Then, using the words you have selected, fill in the blank spaces in the story.

Now you've created your own hilarious MAD LIBS® game!

WHY DO SKUNKS SMELL?

NOUN _____

ADJECTIVE _____

PLURAL NOUN _____

A PLACE _____

PLURAL NOUN _____

ADJECTIVE _____

NOUN _____

VERB ENDING IN "ING" _____

PART OF THE BODY _____

PART OF THE BODY (PLURAL) _____

PART OF THE BODY (PLURAL) _____

ADVERB _____

COLOR _____

PART OF THE BODY _____

PART OF THE BODY _____

MAD LIBS
WHY DO SKUNKS SMELL?

Surprisingly, a skunk is a friendly _____ who can make a/an
                                        NOUN

_____ household pet. But what makes these _____
   ADJECTIVE   PLURAL NOUN

smell to high (the) _____? The skunk has scent _____
                        A PLACE   PLURAL NOUN

that contain a/an _____-smelling fluid. When attacked, the
                     ADJECTIVE

skunk aims this smelly _____ at its enemies. But the skunk does
                           NOUN

give warning before _____. It raises its _____
                       VERB ENDING IN "ING"   PART OF THE BODY

first, or stamps its _____ so that you can run away as fast
                        PART OF THE BODY (PLURAL)

as your _____ can carry you. The most _____
            PART OF THE BODY (PLURAL)   ADVERB

recognizable skunk is the one with a _____ line on its _____
                                         COLOR   PART OF THE BODY

and another one between its _____ and its ears.
                               PART OF THE BODY

MAD LIBS® is fun to play with friends, but you can also play it by yourself! To begin with, DO NOT look at the story on the page below. Fill in the blanks on this page with the words called for. Then, using the words you have selected, fill in the blank spaces in the story.

Now you've created your own hilarious MAD LIBS® game!

FAMOUS QUOTES FROM THE AMERICAN REVOLUTION

NOUN _____

NOUN _____

COLOR _____

PART OF THE BODY (PLURAL) _____

NOUN _____

PLURAL NOUN _____

VERB ENDING IN "ING" _____

NOUN _____

PLURAL NOUN _____

PLURAL NOUN _____

ADJECTIVE _____

NOUN _____

MAD LIBS
FAMOUS QUOTES FROM
THE AMERICAN REVOLUTION

Nathan Hale said: "I regret that I have but one _____ to give for
NOUN

my _____."
NOUN

William Prescott said: "Don't fire until you see the _____ of their
COLOR

_____."
PART OF THE BODY (PLURAL)

Patrick Henry said: "Give me liberty or give me _____.
NOUN

Paul Revere said: "The _____ are _____."
PLURAL NOUN VERB ENDING IN "ING"

John Hancock said: "I wrote my _____ large so the king could
NOUN

read it without his _____."
PLURAL NOUN

Thomas Jefferson said: "All _____ are created equal. They are
PLURAL NOUN

endowed by their creator with certain _____ rights and among
ADJECTIVE

these are life, liberty, and the pursuit of _____."
NOUN

MAD LIBS®

SLEEPOVER PARTY
MAD LIBS

concept created by Roger Price and Leonard Stern

INSTRUCTIONS

MAD LIBS® is a game for people who don't like games!
It can be played by one, two, three, four, or forty.

● RIDICULOUSLY SIMPLE DIRECTIONS

In this tablet you will find stories containing blank spaces where words are left out. One player, the READER, selects one of these stories. The READER does not tell anyone what the story is about. Instead, he/she asks the other players, the WRITERS, to give him/her words. These words are used to fill in the blank spaces in the story.

● TO PLAY

The READER asks each WRITER in turn to call out a word—an adjective or a noun or whatever the space calls for—and uses them to fill in the blank spaces in the story. The result is a MAD LIBS® game.

When the READER then reads the completed MAD LIBS® game to the other players, they will discover that they have written a story that is fantastic, screamingly funny, shocking, silly, crazy, or just plain dumb—depending upon which words each WRITER called out.

● EXAMPLE (*Before* and *After*)

"_____!" he said _____
    EXCLAMATION   ADVERB

as he jumped into his convertible _____ and
                                  NOUN

drove off with his _____ wife.
               ADJECTIVE

"_____*Ouch*_____!" he said _____*stupidly*_____
    EXCLAMATION   ADVERB

as he jumped into his convertible _____*cat*_____ and
                                  NOUN

drove off with his _____*brave*_____ wife.
               ADJECTIVE

QUICK REVIEW

In case you have forgotten what adjectives, adverbs, nouns, and verbs are, here is a quick review:

An ADJECTIVE describes something or somebody. *Lumpy, soft, ugly, messy,* and *short* are adjectives.

An ADVERB tells how something is done. It modifies a verb and usually ends in "ly." *Modestly, stupidly, greedily,* and *carefully* are adverbs.

A NOUN is the name of a person, place, or thing. *Sidewalk, umbrella, bridle, bathtub,* and *nose* are nouns.

A VERB is an action word. *Run, pitch, jump,* and *swim* are verbs. Put the verbs in past tense if the directions say PAST TENSE. *Ran, pitched, jumped,* and *swam* are verbs in the past tense.

When we ask for A PLACE, we mean any sort of place: a country or city *(Spain, Cleveland)* or a room *(bathroom, kitchen).*

An EXCLAMATION or SILLY WORD is any sort of funny sound, gasp, grunt, or outcry, like *Wow!, Ouch!, Whomp!, Ick!,* and *Gadzooks!*

When we ask for specific words, like a NUMBER, a COLOR, an ANIMAL, or a PART OF THE BODY, we mean a word that is one of those things, like *seven, blue, horse,* or *head.*

When we ask for a PLURAL, it means more than one. For example, *cat* pluralized is *cats.*

MAD LIBS® is fun to play with friends, but you can also play it by yourself! To begin with, DO NOT look at the story on the page below. Fill in the blanks on this page with the words called for. Then, using the words you have selected, fill in the blank spaces in the story.

Now you've created your own hilarious MAD LIBS® game!

YOU'RE INVITED

_____ PERSON IN ROOM (FEMALE)

_____ ADJECTIVE

_____ NOUN

_____ NOUN

_____ CELEBRITY

_____ ADVERB

_____ NUMBER

_____ ADJECTIVE

_____ NOUN

_____ NOUN

_____ PART OF THE BODY

_____ PLURAL NOUN

_____ ADJECTIVE

_____ PLURAL NOUN

_____ PLURAL NOUN

_____ ADJECTIVE

_____ PLURAL NOUN

_____ LETTER OF THE ALPHABET

_____ CELEBRITY

_____ SAME CELEBRITY

_____ ADJECTIVE

MAD LIBS

YOU'RE INVITED

Dear _____,

PERSON IN ROOM (FEMALE)

I would like to invite you to a/an _____ sleepover party this

ADJECTIVE

Friday night at my _____. I live on the corner of South

NOUN

_____ Street and _____ Lane. Please arrive _____

NOUN   CELEBRITY   ADVERB

at _____ o'clock. Don't forget to bring a/an _____

NUMBER   ADJECTIVE

sleeping _____ and a soft _____ to rest your

NOUN   NOUN

_____ on. We'll have pizza topped with _____ for

PART OF THE BODY   PLURAL NOUN

dinner, and we'll watch a/an _____ movie. When it is time for

ADJECTIVE

bed, we'll all change into our _____ and turn out the

PLURAL NOUN

_____. Then we'll tell _____ ghost stories and talk

PLURAL NOUN   ADJECTIVE

about all the cute _____ at school! Please RSV-

PLURAL NOUN

_____ to me by e-mail at iluv-_____@_____.

LETTER OF THE ALPHABET   CELEBRITY   SAME CELEBRITY

com. Hope you can join our _____ party!

ADJECTIVE

LET'S GET PACKING!

_____ NOUN

_____ ADJECTIVE

_____ NOUN

_____ ADJECTIVE

_____ PLURAL NOUN

_____ NOUN

_____ PART OF THE BODY (PLURAL)

_____ VERB

_____ ADJECTIVE

_____ CELEBRITY

_____ VERB

_____ ADVERB

_____ ADJECTIVE

_____ NOUN

_____ VERB

_____ VERB ENDING IN "ING"

_____ NOUN

_____ ADJECTIVE

MAD LIBS
LET'S GET PACKING!

If you are going to a sleepover at a friend's _____, here's a/an
                            NOUN

_____ list of things to put in your overnight _____:
ADJECTIVE   NOUN

1. _____ pajamas and a change of _____ for the next day.
   ADJECTIVE   PLURAL NOUN

2. A tooth-_____ for brushing your _____.
          NOUN   PART OF THE BODY (PLURAL)

3. Some CDs so you and your friends can _____ to your favorite
                               VERB

_____ tunes.
ADJECTIVE

4. Magazines with someone like _____ on the cover and articles
                      CELEBRITY

about how to _____ _____.
          VERB   ADVERB

5. A/An _____ _____-light will help you to
        ADJECTIVE   NOUN

_____ in the dark while you stay up _____
   VERB   VERB ENDING IN "ING"

into the wee hours of the _____.
                     NOUN

If you follow this checklist, you should have a really _____
                                     ADJECTIVE

sleepover.

MAD LIBS® is fun to play with friends, but you can also play it by yourself! To begin with, DO NOT look at the story on the page below. Fill in the blanks on this page with the words called for. Then, using the words you have selected, fill in the blank spaces in the story.

Now you've created your own hilarious MAD LIBS® game!

PILLOW FIGHT!

ADJECTIVE _____

PERSON IN ROOM (FEMALE) _____

ADJECTIVE _____

NOUN _____

PART OF THE BODY _____

NOUN _____

PERSON IN ROOM (FEMALE) _____

PART OF THE BODY (PLURAL) _____

NOUN _____

PLURAL NOUN _____

ADJECTIVE _____

ADJECTIVE _____

ADJECTIVE _____

MAD LIBS
PILLOW FIGHT!

The last time I went to a sleepover, a/an _____ pillow fight
ADJECTIVE

broke out. Out of nowhere, _____ grabbed her
PERSON IN ROOM (FEMALE)

_____, fluffy _____ and began swinging it at anyone
ADJECTIVE   _NOUN_

close to her. Soon, everyone else joined in! At one point, I got hit right in the

back of my _____. As soon as I recovered, I tossed my
PART OF THE BODY

_____ at _____'s _____, but I
NOUN   _PERSON IN ROOM (FEMALE)_   _PART OF THE BODY (PLURAL)_

missed. Instead, I knocked over an expensive _____ and my pillow
NOUN

split open! _____ flew everywhere, covering the room in a layer of
PLURAL NOUN

_____ feathers. The fighting stopped when we all broke out in
ADJECTIVE

_____ laughter. The fun ended when we realized we had to clean
ADJECTIVE

up the _____ mess!
ADJECTIVE

MAD LIBS® is fun to play with friends, but you can also play it by yourself! To begin with, DO NOT look at the story on the page below. Fill in the blanks on this page with the words called for. Then, using the words you have selected, fill in the blank spaces in the story.

Now you've created your own hilarious MAD LIBS® game!

SLEEPWALKING

VERB ENDING IN "ING" _____

ADJECTIVE _____

PLURAL NOUN _____

PLURAL NOUN _____

VERB _____

PART OF THE BODY (PLURAL) _____

VERB _____

ADJECTIVE _____

NOUN _____

NOUN _____

PLURAL NOUN _____

ADJECTIVE _____

NOUN _____

SILLY WORD _____

PLURAL NOUN _____

MAD LIBS

SLEEPWALKING

Sleep-_____ is a/an _____ phenomenon that a
    VERB ENDING IN "ING"   ADJECTIVE

surprising number of _____ experience. Usually, sleepwalkers
              PLURAL NOUN

climb out of their _____ and begin to _____ with
       PLURAL NOUN   VERB

their _____ tightly shut. Sometimes they _____
    PART OF THE BODY (PLURAL)   VERB

outdoors wearing only their _____ pajamas. And it's not
              ADJECTIVE

uncommon for _____-walkers to raid the _____ and eat
       NOUN   NOUN

lots of _____. What's truly amazing is that they don't remember
    PLURAL NOUN

a/an _____ thing the following _____. They'll open
    ADJECTIVE   NOUN

the fridge and say, "_____! Where did all the _____
       SILLY WORD   PLURAL NOUN

go?" They may never know!

M.A.S.H.

ADJECTIVE

_____

NUMBER

_____

PLURAL NOUN

_____

A PLACE

_____

PERSON IN ROOM (MALE)

_____

ADJECTIVE

_____

A PLACE

_____

ADJECTIVE

_____

ADJECTIVE

_____

NOUN

_____

A PLACE

_____

ADJECTIVE

_____

NUMBER

_____

NOUN

_____

NUMBER

_____

OCCUPATION

_____

NOUN

_____

ADJECTIVE

_____

MAD LIBS® is fun to play with friends, but you can also play it by yourself! To begin with, DO NOT look at the story on the page below. Fill in the blanks on this page with the words called for. Then, using the words you have selected, fill in the blank spaces in the story.

Now you've created your own hilarious MAD LIBS® game!

MAD LIBS
M.A.S.H.

Congratulations! According to M.A.S.H. (the ultimate sleepover game), your

future looks bright and _____. When you are _____
　　　　　　　　　　　　　　　ADJECTIVE　　　　　　　　　　　　NUMBER

years old, you will meet the man of your _____ at (the)
　　　　　　　　　　　　　　　　　　　　　　　PLURAL NOUN

_____. His name will be _____. You will have
　　　A PLACE　　　　　　　　　　　　PERSON IN ROOM (MALE)

a/an _____ wedding, and you will go to (the)
　　　　ADJECTIVE

_____ on your _____ honeymoon. When you
　　A PLACE　　　　　　　　　　ADJECTIVE

return, you will move into a/an _____ _____ in (the)
　　　　　　　　　　　　　　　　　ADJECTIVE　　　　　NOUN

_____. You will drive a/an _____ car. Then,
　　A PLACE　　　　　　　　　　　　　　ADJECTIVE

when you have been married for _____years, you will have your first
　　　　　　　　　　　　　　　　NUMBER

_____. You will go on to have _____more children. You
　NOUN　　　　　　　　　　　　　　　NUMBER

will work as a/an _____until you retire and move to a tropical
　　　　　　　　　OCCUPATION

_____. Your M.A.S.H. future looks prosperous and
　　NOUN

_____, so prepare to enjoy it!
　ADJECTIVE

MAD LIBS® is fun to play with friends, but you can also play it by yourself! To begin with, DO NOT look at the story on the page below. Fill in the blanks on this page with the words called for. Then, using the words you have selected, fill in the blank spaces in the story.

Now you've created your own hilarious MAD LIBS® game!

PRANKS FOR NOTHING

_____ ADJECTIVE

_____ ADJECTIVE

_____ PLURAL NOUN

_____ ADJECTIVE

_____ PLURAL NOUN

_____ PLURAL NOUN

_____ ADJECTIVE

_____ VERB ENDING IN "ING"

_____ NOUN

_____ NOUN

_____ ADJECTIVE

_____ NOUN

_____ ADJECTIVE

_____ PART OF THE BODY

_____ ADJECTIVE

_____ PLURAL NOUN

_____ PART OF THE BODY (PLURAL)

_____ ADJECTIVE

_____ PART OF THE BODY (PLURAL)

_____ COLOR

MAD LIBS
PRANKS FOR NOTHING

Whenever my _____ sister and her _____
                    ADJECTIVE   ADJECTIVE

_____ have a sleepover party, I love to play _____
PLURAL NOUN   ADJECTIVE

pranks on them. Once, I put gummy _____ in everyone's sleeping
                                   PLURAL NOUN

_____. They thought they were _____ bugs, and they
PLURAL NOUN   ADJECTIVE

were out of their _____ bags in record time! Another time, I
                  VERB ENDING IN "ING"

hid all the rolls of _____ paper in the trunk of Dad's
                       NOUN

_____, not knowing that Dad, a/an _____ doctor, was
   NOUN   ADJECTIVE

on duty at the _____ that night. But the most _____
                 NOUN   ADJECTIVE

prank of all time was when I replaced all of the _____-paste
                                                 PART OF THE BODY

with _____ icing. When my sister's _____ brushed
      ADJECTIVE   PLURAL NOUN

their _____ with it, the _____ looks on
      PART OF THE BODY (PLURAL)   ADJECTIVE

their _____ were priceless—but the _____
      PART OF THE BODY (PLURAL)   COLOR

icing all over their teeth was even better!

MAD LIBS® is fun to play with friends, but you can also play it by yourself! To begin with, DO NOT look at the story on the page below. Fill in the blanks on this page with the words called for. Then, using the words you have selected, fill in the blank spaces in the story.

Now you've created your own hilarious MAD LIBS® game!

LIGHT AS A FEATHER

_____ ADJECTIVE

_____ ADJECTIVE

_____ ADJECTIVE

_____ ADJECTIVE

_____ NOUN

_____ PLURAL NOUN

_____ PART OF THE BODY (PLURAL)

_____ ADVERB

_____ ADJECTIVE

_____ NUMBER

_____ NOUN

_____ NOUN

_____ NOUN

_____ ADVERB

_____ NOUN

_____ NOUN

_____ ADVERB

_____ PLURAL NOUN

_____ ADJECTIVE

MAD LIBS
LIGHT AS A FEATHER

Another _____ sleepover game is _____ as a feather,
         ADJECTIVE   ADJECTIVE

_____ as a board. You'll need a/an _____ volunteer
   ADJECTIVE   ADJECTIVE

to lie down on the _____ with her _____ closed and her
                        NOUN   PLURAL NOUN

_____ folded across her chest. Tell her to breathe
   PART OF THE BODY (PLURAL)

_____ and remain _____ and relaxed. Then gather
     ADVERB   ADJECTIVE

in a circle around her, placing _____ fingers underneath her
                                     NUMBER

_____ as you repeat the phrase, "Light as a/an _____,
     NOUN   NOUN

stiff as a/an _____." On the count of three, _____ lift
                   NOUN   ADVERB

her off the _____ and raise her to the _____. Then
                 NOUN   NOUN

lower her down _____. Your _____ will be completely
                    ADVERB   PLURAL NOUN

amazed at this _____ feat!
                   ADJECTIVE

MAD LIBS® is fun to play with friends, but you can also play it by yourself! To begin with, DO NOT look at the story on the page below. Fill in the blanks on this page with the words called for. Then, using the words you have selected, fill in the blank spaces in the story.

Now you've created your own hilarious MAD LIBS® game!

LET'S DANCE!

_____
ADJECTIVE

_____
PLURAL NOUN

_____
NUMBER

_____
PLURAL NOUN

_____
ADJECTIVE

_____
ADVERB

_____
ADJECTIVE

_____
NOUN

_____
VERB (PAST TENSE)

_____
PART OF THE BODY

_____
PERSON IN ROOM

_____
ADJECTIVE

_____
NUMBER

_____
PART OF THE BODY

_____
ADVERB

_____
ADJECTIVE

_____
PLURAL NOUN

_____
ADVERB

_____
PLURAL NOUN

_____
NOUN

_____
PART OF THE BODY (PLURAL)

MAD LIB
LET'S DANCE!

At my _____ sleepover party, my best _____ and I
        ADJECTIVE   PLURAL NOUN

decided to have a dance-off. We made my _____-year-old little sister
                                    NUMBER

be the judge. We broke into two teams, "The _____" and "The
                                       PLURAL NOUN

_____ Dancers." My team danced _____, but the
  ADJECTIVE   ADVERB

other team's _____ moves were out of this _____!
           ADJECTIVE   NOUN

They totally out-_____ us. So when no one was looking, I
               VERB (PAST TENSE)

grabbed my sister by the _____ and pulled her aside.
                        PART OF THE BODY

"_____," I whispered, "I promise to do all of your
  PERSON IN ROOM

_____ chores for _____ months if you say that my team
  ADJECTIVE   NUMBER

won." My sister shook her _____. "No way!" she said
                       PART OF THE BODY

_____. "Your team danced worse than a bunch of
  ADVERB

_____ _____!" "Fine," I said. "Then I'll just have to
  ADJECTIVE   PLURAL NOUN

tell all of my friends that you're _____ afraid of _____."
                             ADVERB   PLURAL NOUN

That helped to change her _____. We won that contest,
                        NOUN

_____ down!
  PART OF THE BODY (PLURAL)

From SLEEPOVER PARTY MAD LIBS® • Copyright © 2008 by Penguin Random House LLC.

SNORE NO MORE

_____ ADJECTIVE

_____ NOUN

_____ NOUN

_____ ADJECTIVE

_____ VERB ENDING IN "ING"

_____ VERB

_____ PART OF THE BODY

_____ VERB ENDING IN "ING"

_____ ADJECTIVE

_____ ADJECTIVE

_____ ADJECTIVE

_____ VERB ENDING IN "ING"

_____ ADJECTIVE

_____ ADJECTIVE

_____ PART OF THE BODY

MAD LIBS
SNORE NO MORE

Snoring is a loud and often _____ sound that can be compared
ADJECTIVE

to sawing a piece of _____ or to a freight _____ roaring
NOUN   NOUN

down the tracks. Fortunately, there are many _____ solutions to
ADJECTIVE

keep a snorer from _____:
VERB ENDING IN "ING"

1. _____ on your _____ instead of on your back.
VERB   PART OF THE BODY

2. Try _____ without a/an _____ pillow.
VERB ENDING IN "ING"   ADJECTIVE

3. Learn to play the didgeridoo, a/an _____
ADJECTIVE

Australian wind instrument. Studies have shown that this strengthens

_____ airways and helps reduce _____. The
ADJECTIVE   VERB ENDING IN "ING"

trouble with this _____ solution is that most people can't stand
ADJECTIVE

the _____ sound of the didgeridoo.
ADJECTIVE

4. If all else fails and the snoring continues, buy a pair of

_____-plugs for anyone sleeping nearby!
PART OF THE BODY

MAD LIBS® is fun to play with friends, but you can also play it by yourself! To begin with, DO NOT look at the story on the page below. Fill in the blanks on this page with the words called for. Then, using the words you have selected, fill in the blank spaces in the story.

Now you've created your own hilarious MAD LIBS® game!

PIZZA PARTY

CELEBRITY _____

ADJECTIVE _____

NUMBER _____

ADJECTIVE _____

PLURAL NOUN _____

PLURAL NOUN _____

NOUN _____

ADJECTIVE _____

PLURAL NOUN _____

PLURAL NOUN _____

ADJECTIVE _____

PLURAL NOUN _____

PLURAL NOUN _____

NOUN _____

MAD LIBS
PIZZA PARTY

CLERK: Hello, _____'s Pizza Shop. How can I help you?
  CELEBRITY

GIRL: I'm having a/an _____ party, and I would like to order
  ADJECTIVE

enough pizza for _____ _____ people.
  NUMBER   ADJECTIVE

CLERK: Five large _____ should be enough. What
  PLURAL NOUN

_____would you like on them? Tonight's special is pizza topped
  PLURAL NOUN

with _____ cheese, _____ tomatoes, and green
  NOUN   ADJECTIVE

_____.
  PLURAL NOUN

GIRL: Can you add sliced _____ and _____ onions, too?
  PLURAL NOUN   ADJECTIVE

CLERK: Can do. Since you're ordering more than fifty _____'
  PLURAL NOUN

worth of food, you get free _____ for dessert.
  PLURAL NOUN

GIRL: Thanks. And please hurry. We're so hungry, we could eat a/an

_____!
  NOUN

MAD LIBS® is fun to play with friends, but you can also play it by yourself! To begin with, DO NOT look at the story on the page below. Fill in the blanks on this page with the words called for. Then, using the words you have selected, fill in the blank spaces in the story.

Now you've created your own hilarious MAD LIBS® game!

NO BOYS ALLOWED!

PERSON IN ROOM (MALE) _____

ADJECTIVE _____

NOUN _____

PLURAL NOUN _____

ADJECTIVE _____

ADJECTIVE _____

ADJECTIVE _____

PART OF THE BODY _____

PLURAL NOUN _____

PART OF THE BODY (PLURAL) _____

PLURAL NOUN _____

Attention, _____! _____ boys are NOT allowed
     PERSON IN ROOM (MALE)   ADJECTIVE

to enter this room. This ESPECIALLY goes for _____-faced
     NOUN

brothers like you! There is a/an _____-only _____
     PLURAL NOUN   ADJECTIVE

party in progress, and you are not invited. If you dare enter, be aware that

you are a target for _____ pranks. We may even subject you to a/an
     ADJECTIVE

_____ makeover and put makeup on your _____
     ADJECTIVE   PART OF THE BODY

before we let you escape. So, if you are made of _____ and snails
     PLURAL NOUN

and puppy-dog _____, please go back to where you
     PART OF THE BODY (PLURAL)

came from. No _____ allowed!
     PLURAL NOUN

MIDNIGHT MOVIES

_____ ADJECTIVE

_____ ADJECTIVE

_____ PERSON IN ROOM (FEMALE)

_____ NOUN

_____ ADJECTIVE

_____ NOUN

_____ PLURAL NOUN

_____ ADJECTIVE

_____ ADJECTIVE

_____ NOUN

_____ NOUN

_____ PART OF THE BODY

_____ PLURAL NOUN

_____ PERSON IN ROOM (FEMALE)

_____ NOUN

_____ NOUN

_____ ADJECTIVE

_____ NOUN

MIDNIGHT MOVIES

Looking for the perfect movie to watch at your sleepover? Try one of these

_____ party favorites:
ADJECTIVE

• _____ *Girls:* This film stars _____
  ADJECTIVE   PERSON IN ROOM (FEMALE)

Lohan as a homeschooled _____ who goes to a/an _____
                            NOUN   ADJECTIVE

high school for the first time. Will she turn into a mean _____ like
                                                              NOUN

the rest of the popular _____?
                          PLURAL NOUN

• *Legally* _____: In this movie, a/an _____ sorority
            ADJECTIVE   ADJECTIVE

_____ follows her ex-boyfriend to an Ivy _____ school in an
  NOUN   NOUN

attempt to win back his _____.
                          PART OF THE BODY

• *The Princess* _____: When _____ Thermopolis
                 PLURAL NOUN   PERSON IN ROOM (FEMALE)

discovers she is a/an _____ and an heir to the _____ of a/an
                        NOUN   NOUN

_____ country, her entire _____ is turned upside down.
ADJECTIVE   NOUN

MAD LIBS® is fun to play with friends, but you can also play it by yourself! To begin with, DO NOT look at the story on the page below. Fill in the blanks on this page with the words called for. Then, using the words you have selected, fill in the blank spaces in the story.

Now you've created your own hilarious MAD LIBS® game!

A GHASTLY GHOST STORY (PART 1)

ADJECTIVE _____

PLURAL NOUN _____

NOUN _____

NOUN _____

ADJECTIVE _____

PLURAL NOUN _____

NOUN _____

VERB (PAST TENSE) _____

ADJECTIVE _____

NOUN _____

ADJECTIVE _____

PART OF THE BODY (PLURAL) _____

MAD LIBS
A GHASTLY GHOST STORY
(PART 1)

One dark and _____ night I had a sleepover party with seven
                    ADJECTIVE

_____ at my family's old Victorian _____ at the edge of
   PLURAL NOUN   NOUN

town. I was the first person in the house to fall asleep, and in the middle of

the _____, I was startled awake by a/an _____ sound
        NOUN   ADJECTIVE

coming from the attic. I couldn't stop my _____ from shaking as I
                                             PLURAL NOUN

slipped into a/an _____, _____ upstairs, and
                     NOUN   VERB (PAST TENSE)

opened the door to the attic. Out of nowhere, a/an _____ figure
                                                        ADJECTIVE

in a pale white _____ with long _____ hair flew past
                    NOUN   ADJECTIVE

me. Terrified, I screamed at the top of my _____.
                                              PART OF THE BODY (PLURAL)

A GHASTLY GHOST STORY
(PART 2)

NOUN _____

VERB ENDING IN "ING" _____

NOUN _____

PLURAL NOUN _____

NOUN _____

PART OF THE BODY _____

PLURAL NOUN _____

PLURAL NOUN _____

ADJECTIVE _____

ADJECTIVE _____

ADVERB _____

NOUN _____

NOUN _____

"Relax," said the _____.

NOUN
"You're _____ like a leaf,

VERB ENDING IN "ING"

but you need not be afraid. I am a friendly _____."

NOUN
"Really?"

I said. "Wow! I can't wait for you to meet my _____."

PLURAL NOUN

"I would love to, but unfortunately I can only reveal myself to the first

_____ who falls asleep," the ghost replied. And in the blink of a/an

NOUN

_____, the ghost was gone. I ran to awaken my sleeping

PART OF THE BODY

_____ to tell them what had happened, but they said they didn't

PLURAL NOUN

believe me. They told me I'd lost all my _____! But I could tell

PLURAL NOUN

they wished they had seen the _____ ghost. Sure enough, the

ADJECTIVE

next time I had a sleepover at my _____ house, each girl tried

ADJECTIVE

_____ to be the first _____ to fall asleep and meet the

ADVERB   NOUN

friendly _____!

NOUN

MAD LIBS® is fun to play with friends, but you can also play it by yourself! To begin with, DO NOT look at the story on the page below. Fill in the blanks on this page with the words called for. Then, using the words you have selected, fill in the blank spaces in the story.

Now you've created your own hilarious MAD LIBS® game!

HOT FUDGE SUNDAES

NOUN _____

NUMBER _____

PLURAL NOUN _____

ADJECTIVE _____

ADJECTIVE _____

ADJECTIVE _____

NOUN _____

NUMBER _____

PLURAL NOUN _____

NOUN _____

NOUN _____

NOUN _____

VERB (PAST TENSE) _____

PLURAL NOUN _____

ADJECTIVE _____

VERB _____

Making a hot fudge _____ is as simple as one, two,
NOUN

_____. All you need are the following _____:
NUMBER   PLURAL NOUN

A pint of _____ ice cream
ADJECTIVE

1 jar of _____ fudge sauce
ADJECTIVE

1 cup of _____ nuts
ADJECTIVE

1 can of whipped _____
NOUN

_____ maraschino _____
NUMBER   PLURAL NOUN

Scoop the ice _____ into a glass _____. Pour on a
NOUN   NOUN

generous portion of hot _____ sauce, and add a heaping mound of
NOUN

_____ cream. Sprinkle with _____ and top off with
VERB (PAST TENSE)   PLURAL NOUN

a/an _____ cherry. Now _____ and enjoy!
ADJECTIVE   VERB

MAD LIBS® is fun to play with friends, but you can also play it by yourself! To begin with, DO NOT look at the story on the page below. Fill in the blanks on this page with the words called for. Then, using the words you have selected, fill in the blank spaces in the story.

Now you've created your own hilarious MAD LIBS® game!

TRUTH OR DARE (PART 1)

_____ NOUN

_____ PERSON IN ROOM (MALE)

_____ NOUN

_____ NUMBER

_____ VERB (PAST TENSE)

_____ NOUN

_____ NUMBER

_____ ADJECTIVE

_____ VERB

_____ NOUN

_____ ADJECTIVE

_____ NOUN

_____ ADJECTIVE

_____ TYPE OF LIQUID

_____ NOUN

_____ PLURAL NOUN

_____ TYPE OF LIQUID

MAD LIBS®
TRUTH OR DARE (PART 1)

Let's play truth or dare! First, some truths:

Q: What is the name of the _____ you like?
NOUN

A: _____.
PERSON IN ROOM (MALE)

Q: What is one _____ no one knows about you?
NOUN

A: When I was _____ years old, I _____ like a/an
NUMBER   VERB (PAST TENSE)

_____ in front of _____ people.
NOUN   NUMBER

Q: If you were stranded on a/an _____ island, what three things
ADJECTIVE

would you bring with you?

A: I couldn't _____ without my precious _____,
VERB   NOUN

my _____ _____, and a/an _____ bottle
ADJECTIVE   NOUN   ADJECTIVE

of _____.
TYPE OF LIQUID

Q: What is the strangest _____ you have ever eaten?
NOUN

A: _____ dipped in _____.
PLURAL NOUN   TYPE OF LIQUID

MAD LIBS® is fun to play with friends, but you can also play it by yourself! To begin with, DO NOT look at the story on the page below. Fill in the blanks on this page with the words called for. Then, using the words you have selected, fill in the blank spaces in the story.

Now you've created your own hilarious MAD LIBS® game!

TRUTH OR DARE (PART 2)

_____ ADJECTIVE

_____ VERB

_____ NOUN

_____ ADJECTIVE

_____ ADJECTIVE

_____ NOUN

_____ NOUN

_____ VERB

_____ PLURAL NOUN

_____ ADJECTIVE

_____ PART OF THE BODY (PLURAL)

_____ NUMBER

MAD LIBS
TRUTH OR DARE (PART 2)

And now for the dares!

DARE: Pretend you are a/an _____ puppy. _____
            ADJECTIVE   VERB

loudly and wag your _____.
                          NOUN

DARE: Put on some _____ music and dance like
                              ADJECTIVE

a/an _____ _____ for one minute.
        ADJECTIVE   NOUN

DARE: Hop on one _____ while you _____ and say
                        NOUN   VERB

the alphabet backward.

DARE: Take off your socks and _____ and step into the shower.
                                    PLURAL NOUN

Then turn on the _____ water and yodel at the top of your
                          ADJECTIVE

_____ for _____ seconds.
   PART OF THE BODY (PLURAL)   NUMBER

MAD LIBS® is fun to play with friends, but you can also play it by yourself! To begin with, DO NOT look at the story on the page below. Fill in the blanks on this page with the words called for. Then, using the words you have selected, fill in the blank spaces in the story.

Now you've created your own hilarious MAD LIBS® game!

A BAD NIGHTMARE

_____ PERSON IN ROOM (FEMALE)

_____ ADJECTIVE

_____ PLURAL NOUN

_____ NOUN

_____ PLURAL NOUN

_____ PLURAL NOUN

_____ ADVERB

_____ PART OF THE BODY (PLURAL)

_____ NOUN

_____ NOUN

_____ SAME NOUN

_____ VERB ENDING IN "ING"

_____ VERB ENDING IN "ING"

MAD LIBS

A BAD NIGHTMARE

One night when I slept over at my friend _____'s house I had
                                     PERSON IN ROOM (FEMALE)

a/an _____ nightmare that scared the living _____ out
         ADJECTIVE   PLURAL NOUN

of me. I dreamed I was in school, standing in front of my English

_____, giving a report on Shakespeare's _____, when I
     NOUN   PLURAL NOUN

realized I wasn't wearing any _____. Embarrassed beyond belief, I
                                PLURAL NOUN

_____ put my hands over my _____ and
     ADVERB   PART OF THE BODY (PLURAL)

ran out of the classroom at breakneck _____. Suddenly, I was being
                                          NOUN

chased by a wild _____! Just as the _____ was about to
                    NOUN   SAME NOUN

catch me, I woke up _____ with fright. I spent the rest of the
                      VERB ENDING IN "ING"

night _____ with the light on!
         VERB ENDING IN "ING"

MAD LIBS® is fun to play with friends, but you can also play it by yourself! To begin with, DO NOT look at the story on the page below. Fill in the blanks on this page with the words called for. Then, using the words you have selected, fill in the blank spaces in the story.

Now you've created your own hilarious MAD LIBS® game!

MAKEOVER MADNESS

_____ ADJECTIVE

_____ PERSON IN ROOM (FEMALE)

_____ PERSON IN ROOM (FEMALE)

_____ ADJECTIVE

_____ EXCLAMATION

_____ NOUN

_____ PART OF THE BODY

_____ PART OF THE BODY

_____ ADJECTIVE

_____ PLURAL NOUN

_____ NOUN

_____ COLOR

_____ NOUN

_____ PLURAL NOUN

_____ ADJECTIVE

_____ VERB

_____ ADVERB

_____ PLURAL NOUN

_____ NOUN

_____ PART OF THE BODY (PLURAL)

MAD LIBS

MAKEOVER MADNESS

A/An _____ scene to be played by _____ and
    ADJECTIVE   PERSON IN ROOM (FEMALE)

_____.
PERSON IN ROOM (FEMALE)

GIRL 1: I'm going to give you a/an _____ makeover.
                                    ADJECTIVE

GIRL 2: _____! Will I look like a new _____?
        EXCLAMATION   NOUN

GIRL 1: Yes, from head to _____. First, we'll brush your
                          PART OF THE BODY

_____ to make it sleek and _____.
PART OF THE BODY   ADJECTIVE

GIRL 2: What about my _____? My friends say my eyes are my
                       PLURAL NOUN

best _____.
     NOUN

GIRL 1: They are. Applying _____ eye _____ will
                       COLOR   NOUN

definitely bring out the color of your _____. And changing your
                                  PLURAL NOUN

_____ clothes will also help.
ADJECTIVE

GIRL 2: You don't like the way I _____?
                         VERB

GIRL 1: You should try and dress more _____. Those
                              ADVERB

_____ you've been wearing are so last year. Trust me, when we're
PLURAL NOUN

finished, you'll be the talk of the _____.
                               NOUN

GIRL 2: I've got my _____ crossed!
                   PART OF THE BODY (PLURAL)

MAD LIBS® is fun to play with friends, but you can also play it by yourself! To begin with, DO NOT look at the story on the page below. Fill in the blanks on this page with the words called for. Then, using the words you have selected, fill in the blank spaces in the story.

Now you've created your own hilarious MAD LIBS® game!

HOW TO SING KARAOKE

ADJECTIVE _____

A PLACE _____

ADVERB _____

NOUN _____

ADJECTIVE _____

ADJECTIVE _____

ADJECTIVE _____

ADJECTIVE _____

ADJECTIVE _____

NOUN _____

ADVERB _____

PLURAL NOUN _____

NOUN _____

MAD LIBS

HOW TO SING KARAOKE

Karaoke is a/an _____ form of entertainment that first became
              ADJECTIVE

popular in (the) _____ and _____ caught on all
          A PLACE   ADVERB

over the _____. In karaoke, you sing along to a/an _____
        NOUN   ADJECTIVE

song using a/an _____ microphone. You don't have to be a
           ADJECTIVE

particularly good singer to sing karaoke—you can even be a/an

_____ singer. The most important thing is to have a/an
   ADJECTIVE

_____ time. Karaoke is especially _____ at a
   ADJECTIVE   ADJECTIVE

sleepover party. You don't even need a/an _____ machine! You can
                                NOUN

just turn up the radio and sing _____. Just be sure to give other
                          ADVERB

_____ a turn—you don't want to be a/an _____ hog!
 PLURAL NOUN   NOUN

MAD LIBS® is fun to play with friends, but you can also play it by yourself! To begin with, DO NOT look at the story on the page below. Fill in the blanks on this page with the words called for. Then, using the words you have selected, fill in the blank spaces in the story.

Now you've created your own hilarious MAD LIBS® game!

SLEEPOVER, SCHMEEPOVER

ADJECTIVE_____

PLURAL NOUN _____

NUMBER _____

NOUN _____

NUMBER _____

NOUN _____

NOUN _____

PLURAL NOUN _____

NOUN _____

PLURAL NOUN _____

PLURAL NOUN _____

NOUN _____

PLURAL NOUN _____

ADJECTIVE_____

NOUN _____

MAD LIBS
SLEEPOVER, SCHMEEPOVER

The _____ thing about sleepover parties is that, even though
      ADJECTIVE

you're supposed to "sleep over," chances are you and your _____
          PLURAL NOUN

will catch fewer than _____ winks! It's always the same—you promise
      NUMBER

your mom and _____ that you'll go to bed before _____
     NOUN   NUMBER

o'clock, but instead you stay up until the crack of _____. The next
          NOUN

thing you know, you're waking up to the smell of fried _____ and
         NOUN

scrambled _____ emanating from the _____. After
    PLURAL NOUN   NOUN

breakfast, you change out of your _____, pack your _____,
        PLURAL NOUN   PLURAL NOUN

and stumble into your parents' _____ when they come to pick you
        NOUN

up. If you're like most _____ your age, you'll be so tired, you'll
      PLURAL NOUN

want to take a/an _____ nap the minute you get home. Which
     ADJECTIVE

gets a/an _____ thinking—maybe they should call them awake-
     NOUN

overs instead!

MAD LIBS®

WE WISH YOU A MERRY MAD LIBS

by Roger Price and Leonard Stern

MAD LIBS®

INSTRUCTIONS

MAD LIBS® is a game for people who don't like games!
It can be played by one, two, three, four, or forty.

● RIDICULOUSLY SIMPLE DIRECTIONS

In this tablet you will find stories containing blank spaces where words are left out. One
player, the READER, selects one of these stories. The READER does not tell anyone
what the story is about. Instead, he/she asks the other players, the WRITERS, to give
him/her words. These words are used to fill in the blank spaces in the story.

● TO PLAY

The READER asks each WRITER in turn to call out a word—an adjective or a noun or
whatever the space calls for—and uses them to fill in the blank spaces in the story. The
result is a MAD LIBS® game.

When the READER then reads the completed MAD LIBS® game to the other players,
they will discover that they have written a story that is fantastic, screamingly funny,
shocking, silly, crazy, or just plain dumb—depending upon which words each WRITER
called out.

● EXAMPLE (*Before* and *After*)

"_____!" he said _____
          EXCLAMATION   ADVERB

as he jumped into his convertible _____ and
                                              NOUN

drove off with his _____ wife.
                          ADJECTIVE

"_____*Ouch*_____!" he said _____*stupidly*_____
          EXCLAMATION   ADVERB

as he jumped into his convertible _____*cat*_____ and
                                              NOUN

drove off with his _____*brave*_____ wife.
                          ADJECTIVE

QUICK REVIEW

In case you have forgotten what adjectives, adverbs, nouns, and verbs are, here is a quick review:

An ADJECTIVE describes something or somebody. *Lumpy, soft, ugly, messy,* and *short* are adjectives.

An ADVERB tells how something is done. It modifies a verb and usually ends in "ly." *Modestly, stupidly, greedily,* and *carefully* are adverbs.

A NOUN is the name of a person, place, or thing. *Sidewalk, umbrella, bridle, bathtub,* and *nose* are nouns.

A VERB is an action word. *Run, pitch, jump,* and *swim* are verbs. Put the verbs in past tense if the directions say PAST TENSE. *Ran, pitched, jumped,* and *swam* are verbs in the past tense.

When we ask for A PLACE, we mean any sort of place: a country or city *(Spain, Cleveland)* or a room *(bathroom, kitchen).*

An EXCLAMATION or SILLY WORD is any sort of funny sound, gasp, grunt, or outcry, like *Wow!, Ouch!, Whomp!, Ick!,* and *Gadzooks!*

When we ask for specific words, like a NUMBER, a COLOR, an ANIMAL, or a PART OF THE BODY, we mean a word that is one of those things, like *seven, blue, horse,* or *head.*

When we ask for a PLURAL, it means more than one. For example, *cat* pluralized is *cats.*

VISIT THE NORTH POLE!

_____ ADJECTIVE

_____ ADJECTIVE

_____ NOUN

_____ ADVERB

_____ ADJECTIVE

_____ PART OF THE BODY (PLURAL)

_____ NOUN

_____ PLURAL NOUN

_____ NOUN

_____ ADJECTIVE

_____ ADJECTIVE

_____ ADJECTIVE

_____ PLURAL NOUN

_____ ADJECTIVE

_____ PART OF THE BODY

_____ PLURAL NOUN

MAD LIBS® is fun to play with friends, but you can also play it by yourself! To begin with, DO NOT look at the story on the page below. Fill in the blanks on this page with the words called for. Then, using the words you have selected, fill in the blank spaces in the story.

Now you've created your own hilarious MAD LIBS® game!

Looking for a/an _____ destination for your next vacation? How
ADJECTIVE

about the _____ North Pole? Located in the middle of the Arctic
ADJECTIVE

_____, it is made up of _____ shifting ice, which
NOUN ADVERB

makes it perfect for snowshoeing through the _____ tundra. As
ADJECTIVE

you trek across the ice, keep your _____ peeled for the
PART OF THE BODY (PLURAL)

incredible wildlife that inhabits the North _____—like furry white
NOUN

polar _____, _____ seals, and _____ arctic
PLURAL NOUN NOUN ADJECTIVE

foxes. And when night falls you are in for a/an _____ treat.
ADJECTIVE

You'll be able to see the _____ aurora borealis, otherwise known
ADJECTIVE

as the northern _____. This incredible display of _____
PLURAL NOUN ADJECTIVE

lights will blow your _____. So call 1-800-555-3939 and
PART OF THE BODY

make your travel _____ today!
PLURAL NOUN

MAD LIBS® is fun to play with friends, but you can also play it by yourself! To begin with, DO NOT look at the story on the page below. Fill in the blanks on this page with the words called for. Then, using the words you have selected, fill in the blank spaces in the story.

Now you've created your own hilarious MAD LIBS® game!

SANTA BLOG

_____ ADJECTIVE

_____ ADJECTIVE

_____ NOUN

_____ ADJECTIVE

_____ A PLACE

_____ NOUN

_____ PLURAL NOUN

_____ PLURAL NOUN

_____ ADVERB

_____ NOUN

_____ ADJECTIVE

_____ VERB

_____ VERB

_____ ADJECTIVE

_____ ADJECTIVE

_____ PLURAL NOUN

_____ NOUN

MAD LIBS
SANTA BLOG

Ho, ho, ho, _____ blog fans! Santa here. It's crunch time at my
                    ADJECTIVE

_____ workshop, and everyone is as busy as a/an _____.
     ADJECTIVE   NOUN

I've received tons of _____ letters from girls and boys around
                              ADJECTIVE

(the) _____, and the elves have been working around the
            A PLACE

_____ to make all of their _____. Plus, I've finally
       NOUN   PLURAL NOUN

finished putting together the list of naughty _____, which I'm
                                                      PLURAL NOUN

_____ happy to say is much shorter than last year's! As I look out
        ADVERB

the _____, I can see the reindeer are groomed and look really
        NOUN

_____, and my sleigh is polished and ready to _____. I
     ADJECTIVE   VERB

will be able to _____ through the _____ night sky
                      VERB   ADJECTIVE

as soon as Mrs. Claus finishes letting out my _____ red suit. I'm
                                                    ADJECTIVE

sorry to say, I ate a few too many _____ this past year!
                                      PLURAL NOUN

See you soon! Your _____, Santa
                        NOUN

MAD LIBS® is fun to play with friends, but you can also play it by yourself! To begin with, DO NOT look at the story on the page below. Fill in the blanks on this page with the words called for. Then, using the words you have selected, fill in the blank spaces in the story.

Now you've created your own hilarious MAD LIBS® game!

HOLIDAY WEATHER REPORT

ADJECTIVE _____

PERSON IN ROOM _____

NOUN _____

ADJECTIVE _____

ADJECTIVE _____

NUMBER _____

NOUN _____

NOUN _____

PLURAL NOUN _____

PLURAL NOUN _____

VERB ENDING IN "ING" _____

NUMBER _____

ADJECTIVE _____

PLURAL NOUN _____

VERB _____

NOUN _____

NOUN _____

ADJECTIVE _____

MAD LIBS

HOLIDAY WEATHER REPORT

Good evening, and _____ holidays. I'm _____ with
                   ADJECTIVE   PERSON IN ROOM

your local weather _____. First the good news: We're going to have
                        NOUN

a traditional _____ Christmas. A/An _____
                  ADJECTIVE   ADJECTIVE

snowstorm is heading our way. You can expect three to _____ feet of
                                                           NUMBER

_____ to accumulate before the end of this _____, plus
     NOUN   NOUN

several more _____ of snow by midnight. And you may want to
                PLURAL NOUN

put on your warm _____: Overnight, the temperature is going to
                     PLURAL NOUN

drop below _____ level, with a windchill of negative
              VERB ENDING IN "ING"

_____ degrees. Now the bad news: Driving conditions will be
     NUMBER

extremely _____. I strongly suggest you stay off the _____
              ADJECTIVE   PLURAL NOUN

and _____ at home. Hunker down, light a/an _____
         VERB   NOUN

in the fireplace, and watch the _____-flakes fall. And, most
                                     NOUN

importantly, have a/an _____ Christmas!
                          ADJECTIVE

MAD LIBS® is fun to play with friends, but you can also play it by yourself! To begin with, DO NOT look at the story on the page below. Fill in the blanks on this page with the words called for. Then, using the words you have selected, fill in the blank spaces in the story.

Now you've created your own hilarious MAD LIBS® game!

MOST POPULAR GIFTS

_____ ADJECTIVE

_____ PLURAL NOUN

_____ NOUN

_____ ADJECTIVE

_____ PLURAL NOUN

_____ NOUN

_____ NOUN

_____ NOUN

_____ NOUN

_____ ADJECTIVE

_____ NOUN

_____ PLURAL NOUN

_____ ADJECTIVE

_____ NOUN

_____ ADJECTIVE

_____ NOUN

_____ NOUN

_____ ADJECTIVE

_____ NOUN

MAD LIBS
MOST POPULAR GIFTS

Here is a list of the most _____ gifts for your dear _____:
　　　　　　　　　　　　　　　ADJECTIVE　　　　　　　　　　　　　　　PLURAL NOUN

5. An i-_____. This _____ device can store and play
　　　　　　NOUN　　　　　　　　　ADJECTIVE

up to thirty thousand _____.
　　　　　　　　　　　　PLURAL NOUN

4. A/An _____-cam. Shoot movies or film yourself acting like a/an
　　　　　　NOUN

_____. Then, upload your videos to You-_____,
　　NOUN　　　　　　　　　　　　　　　　　　　　　　　　NOUN

where everyone can see them!

3. *Rock* _____. Ever wanted to be a famous _____?
　　　　　　NOUN　　　　　　　　　　　　　　　　　　　　NOUN

You can act like one with this _____ video game.
　　　　　　　　　　　　　　　ADJECTIVE

2. A flat-screen _____. Watch your favorite movies and TV
　　　　　　　　　NOUN

_____ in _____-definition on an LCD _____.
PLURAL NOUN　　　　ADJECTIVE　　　　　　　　　　　　　　　NOUN

1. If you have _____ friends who are in short supply of self-
　　　　　　　　ADJECTIVE

esteem, buy them a talking _____. With the push of a/an
　　　　　　　　　　　　　　NOUN

_____, it will say things like, "You're so _____!"
　　NOUN　　　　　　　　　　　　　　　　　　　　　　　ADJECTIVE

and "You're the best _____ ever!"
　　　　　　　　　　　NOUN

MAD LIBS® is fun to play with friends, but you can also play it by yourself! To begin with, DO NOT look at the story on the page below. Fill in the blanks on this page with the words called for. Then, using the words you have selected, fill in the blank spaces in the story.

Now you've created your own hilarious MAD LIBS® game!

TAKING CARE OF
YOUR REINDEER

_____ ADJECTIVE

_____ ADJECTIVE

_____ NOUN

_____ ADJECTIVE

_____ NUMBER

_____ ADJECTIVE

_____ PLURAL NOUN

_____ ADJECTIVE

_____ NOUN

_____ ADJECTIVE

_____ NUMBER

_____ ADVERB

_____ ADJECTIVE

_____ NOUN

_____ NOUN

_____ ADVERB

_____ ADJECTIVE

MAD LIBS
TAKING CARE OF YOUR REINDEER

Congratulations! We hear you've adopted a/an _____ reindeer.
_{ADJECTIVE}

They make _____ pets—but they require a lot of care and
_{ADJECTIVE}

_____. Here are some tips for keeping your reindeer happy and
_{NOUN}

_____:
_{ADJECTIVE}

• Feed it _____ times a day. Not difficult to do, as reindeer have a
_{NUMBER}

very _____ diet. They eat grasses, moss, and _____.
_{ADJECTIVE} _{PLURAL NOUN}

• Make sure your reindeer gets _____ exercise. In the wild,
_{ADJECTIVE}

they travel farther than any other land _____. They go on
_{NOUN}

_____ migrations, sometimes covering _____ miles.
_{ADJECTIVE} _{NUMBER}

• Groom your reindeer _____. Its _____ antlers
_{ADVERB} _{ADJECTIVE}

are covered in delicate _____, which you can clean with a soft
_{NOUN}

_____. You should also brush its coat _____ once a month.
_{NOUN} _{ADVERB}

• Take your reindeer to the vet often to make sure it stays healthy

and _____.
_{ADJECTIVE}

From WE WISH YOU A MERRY MAD LIBS® • Copyright © 2010, 2012 by Penguin Random House LLC.

GET TO KNOW MRS. CLAUS

ADJECTIVE _____

NOUN _____

FIRST NAME (FEMALE) _____

NOUN _____

LAST NAME _____

ADJECTIVE _____

PLURAL NOUN _____

PLURAL NOUN _____

NOUN _____

NOUN _____

NOUN _____

NOUN _____

PART OF THE BODY (PLURAL) _____

ADJECTIVE _____

ADJECTIVE _____

ADJECTIVE _____

MAD LIBS® is fun to play with friends, but you can also play it by yourself! To begin with, DO NOT look at the story on the page below. Fill in the blanks on this page with the words called for. Then, using the words you have selected, fill in the blank spaces in the story.

Now you've created your own hilarious MAD LIBS® game!

Here are some _____ facts you may not know about me, Santa

ADJECTIVE

Claus's dear _____:

NOUN

Full name: Mrs. _____ Claus

FIRST NAME (FEMALE)

Hometown: The North _____

NOUN

Activities: Helping my husband, Santa _____, get ready for

LAST NAME

Christmas and taking care of the _____ elves

ADJECTIVE

Interests: Baking Christmas _____ and knitting _____

PLURAL NOUN · PLURAL NOUN

Favorite movies: *It's a Wonderful* _____, *Rudolph the Red-Nosed*

NOUN

_____

NOUN

Favorite books: *The* _____ *Before Christmas, How the*

NOUN

_____ *Stole Christmas*

NOUN

Favorite quotation: "All I want for Christmas is my two front

_____."

PART OF THE BODY (PLURAL)

About me: Have you ever wondered who brings _____ Santa *his*

ADJECTIVE

_____ gifts on Christmas Eve? Well, surprise! It's little,

ADJECTIVE

_____ me!

ADJECTIVE

MAD LIBS® is fun to play with friends, but you can also play it by yourself! To begin with, DO NOT look at the story on the page below. Fill in the blanks on this page with the words called for. Then, using the words you have selected, fill in the blank spaces in the story.

Now you've created your own hilarious MAD LIBS® game!

CHRISTMAS FUNNIES

_____ ADJECTIVE

_____ ADJECTIVE

_____ ADJECTIVE

_____ NOUN

_____ NOUN

_____ ADJECTIVE

_____ NOUN

_____ PLURAL NOUN

_____ ADJECTIVE

_____ FIRST NAME

MAD LIBS®
CHRISTMAS FUNNIES

Q: What do you get when you cross a/an _____ vampire with
ADJECTIVE

a/an _____ snowman?
ADJECTIVE

A: Frostbite!

Q: Why did the _____ reindeer cross the _____?
ADJECTIVE   NOUN

A: To get to the other _____!
NOUN

Q: What do _____ elves sing to Santa?
ADJECTIVE

A: "*Freeze* a Jolly Good _____."
NOUN

Q: What do polar _____ eat for lunch?
PLURAL NOUN

A: *Iceberg*-ers!

Q: What do you call a/an _____ person who is afraid of
ADJECTIVE

_____ Claus?
FIRST NAME

A: *Claus*trophobic.

MAD LIBS® is fun to play with friends, but you can also play it by yourself! To begin with, DO NOT look at the story on the page below. Fill in the blanks on this page with the words called for. Then, using the words you have selected, fill in the blank spaces in the story.

Now you've created your own hilarious MAD LIBS® game!

CHRISTMAS AROUND THE WORLD, PART 1

_____ ADJECTIVE

_____ PLURAL NOUN

_____ NOUN

_____ ADJECTIVE

_____ PLURAL NOUN

_____ ADVERB

_____ NOUN

_____ NOUN

_____ NOUN

_____ PLURAL NOUN

_____ PLURAL NOUN

_____ ADJECTIVE

_____ ADJECTIVE

_____ ADJECTIVE

_____ PLURAL NOUN

_____ PLURAL NOUN

_____ PLURAL NOUN

Americans have many _____ Christmas traditions. They
                              ADJECTIVE

decorate Christmas _____, sing _____ carols, and have
                        PLURAL NOUN   NOUN

_____ Christmas dinners with their families. But how do
ADJECTIVE

_____ around the world celebrate?
PLURAL NOUN

- In **Sweden**, they _____ celebrate San Lucia Day before
                            ADVERB

Christmas. The youngest _____ in the family wears a white
                              NOUN

_____, a red _____, and a crown of _____
NOUN   NOUN   PLURAL NOUN

with candles in it. She then serves coffee and _____ to everyone
                                                    PLURAL NOUN

in her _____ family.
          ADJECTIVE

- In **Australia,** it is hot and _____ at Christmastime, because
                                      ADJECTIVE

this _____ holiday falls in the middle of their summer.
        ADJECTIVE

_____ gather outside at night to light _____ and sing
PLURAL NOUN   PLURAL NOUN

Christmas _____.
              PLURAL NOUN

MAD LIBS® is fun to play with friends, but you can also play it by yourself! To begin with, DO NOT look at the story on the page below. Fill in the blanks on this page with the words called for. Then, using the words you have selected, fill in the blank spaces in the story.

Now you've created your own hilarious MAD LIBS® game!

CHRISTMAS AROUND THE WORLD, PART 2

_____ PLURAL NOUN

_____ NOUN

_____ NOUN

_____ NOUN

_____ PLURAL NOUN

_____ NOUN

_____ ADJECTIVE

_____ PLURAL NOUN

_____ ADJECTIVE

_____ PLURAL NOUN

_____ PLURAL NOUN

_____ ADJECTIVE

_____ ADJECTIVE

_____ PLURAL NOUN

_____ ADJECTIVE

- In **China**, people decorate their _____ homes with paper
ADJECTIVE

_____. They also put up _____ trees decorated with
PLURAL NOUN   ADJECTIVE

_____ lanterns, _____, and red _____.
ADJECTIVE   PLURAL NOUN   PLURAL NOUN

- In **Mexico**, children look forward to a/an _____ party where
ADJECTIVE

young _____ take turns hitting a/an _____ piñata
PLURAL NOUN   ADJECTIVE

with a/an _____, until all the _____ and other treats
NOUN   PLURAL NOUN

fall out.

- In **Germany**, families celebrate the weeks leading up to Christmas with an

Advent _____. Each Sunday, they light another _____
NOUN   NOUN

in the wreath. Before Christmas, Germans celebrate St. Nicholas Day,

where kids put a/an _____ outside their door at night, and in
NOUN

the morning it is filled with candy and _____.
PLURAL NOUN

A TROPICAL CHRISTMAS

PLURAL NOUN _____

NOUN _____

A PLACE _____

PLURAL NOUN _____

ADJECTIVE _____

NOUN _____

NOUN _____

PLURAL NOUN _____

ADJECTIVE _____

ADJECTIVE _____

PLURAL NOUN _____

ADJECTIVE _____

NOUN _____

ADJECTIVE _____

NOUN _____

NOUN _____

ADJECTIVE _____

A TROPICAL CHRISTMAS

Some _____ can't imagine celebrating Christmas where there's no
          PLURAL NOUN

snow falling from the _____. But it's not all bad! Here in (the)
                              NOUN

_____, where it's always sunny, we decorate palm _____
      A PLACE   PLURAL NOUN

with _____ lights instead of decorating a pine _____.
          ADJECTIVE   NOUN

Instead of making a snow-_____, we make _____ out of
                                NOUN   PLURAL NOUN

sand. Best of all, we don't have to bundle up against the _____
                                                                ADJECTIVE

wind and the _____ cold and freeze our _____ off. At
                  ADJECTIVE   PLURAL NOUN

Christmas, we happily splash around in the _____ ocean
                                                  ADJECTIVE

and bask in the _____-shine. Or we go surfing and catch
                      NOUN

_____ waves. As you can see, I no longer dream of a white
      ADJECTIVE

_____. I'm happy celebrating Christmas on a sandy _____
      NOUN   NOUN

in the _____ sun!
            ADJECTIVE

MAD LIBS® is fun to play with friends, but you can also play it by yourself! To begin with, DO NOT look at the story on the page below. Fill in the blanks on this page with the words called for. Then, using the words you have selected, fill in the blank spaces in the story.

Now you've created your own hilarious MAD LIBS® game!

CHRISTMAS IN JULY

LAST NAME _____

ADJECTIVE _____

A PLACE _____

NOUN _____

PLURAL NOUN _____

ADVERB _____

NUMBER _____

ADJECTIVE _____

NOUN _____

NOUN _____

PLURAL NOUN _____

ADJECTIVE _____

VERB _____

NOUN _____

MAD LIBS

CHRISTMAS IN JULY

Hurry on down to _____ Furniture for our _____
             LAST NAME   ADJECTIVE

Christmas-in-July sale! Yes, folks, Christmas has come early here in (the)

_____, and we're celebrating with _____-wide
     A PLACE   NOUN

savings on couches, tables, and _____! With prices _____
                                  PLURAL NOUN   ADVERB

reduced up to _____ percent off, you can't afford to miss this
               NUMBER

_____ event! Purchase any _____ in the store with no
   ADJECTIVE   NOUN

down _____ and no _____ for twelve months. But our
      NOUN   PLURAL NOUN

_____ sale only lasts through Thursday. So don't delay!
   ADJECTIVE

_____ on down today, and have a merry _____ in July!
    VERB   NOUN

MAD LIBS® is fun to play with friends, but you can also play it by yourself! To begin with, DO NOT look at the story on the page below. Fill in the blanks on this page with the words called for. Then, using the words you have selected, fill in the blank spaces in the story.

Now you've created your own hilarious MAD LIBS® game!

ELVES WANTED

_____ PLURAL NOUN

_____ NUMBER

_____ ADJECTIVE

_____ VERB

_____ NOUN

_____ PLURAL NOUN

_____ NOUN

_____ ADJECTIVE

_____ NOUN

_____ ADJECTIVE

_____ ADJECTIVE

_____ VERB

_____ PLURAL NOUN

_____ A PLACE

_____ PART OF THE BODY (PLURAL)

MAD LIBS
ELVES WANTED

Attention, all _____! Santa Claus is looking for _____
         PLURAL NOUN   NUMBER

_____ elves to _____ in his workshop at the North
   ADJECTIVE   VERB

_____. Job responsibilities include making toy _____
    NOUN   PLURAL NOUN

faster than the speed of _____; taking care of eight _____
                              NOUN   ADJECTIVE

reindeer when it is necessary; repairing Santa's shiny, red _____;
                                                                  NOUN

and, of course, sorting letters from _____ girls and boys. Some
                                          ADJECTIVE

very _____ elves might get the chance to _____ in
        ADJECTIVE   VERB

Santa's sleigh on Christmas Eve and help him deliver _____
                                                          PLURAL NOUN

all over (the) _____. Most importantly, candidates'
                  A PLACE

_____ must be full of Christmas cheer!
PART OF THE BODY (PLURAL)

MAD LIBS® is fun to play with friends, but you can also play it by yourself! To begin with, DO NOT look at the story on the page below. Fill in the blanks on this page with the words called for. Then, using the words you have selected, fill in the blank spaces in the story.

Now you've created your own hilarious MAD LIBS® game!

SNOW DAY!

NOUN _____

ADJECTIVE _____

NOUN _____

ADJECTIVE _____

NOUN _____

ADJECTIVE _____

NOUN _____

NOUN _____

NOUN _____

NOUN _____

VERB _____

ADJECTIVE _____

PLURAL NOUN _____

NOUN _____

MAD LIBS
SNOW DAY!

This is your lucky _____. Because of the _____
               NOUN   ADJECTIVE

blizzard, school's been canceled. So how will you spend this unexpected

_____? Here are some _____ suggestions:
   NOUN   ADJECTIVE

- Stay inside and drink hot _____ while watching _____
                              NOUN   ADJECTIVE

cartoons on television.

- Grab your _____ and go sledding down a steep _____.
               NOUN   NOUN

- Find a frozen _____ and go ice-skating on it.
               NOUN

- Build a/an _____ fort. Construct walls out of hard-packed
               NOUN

_____, then _____ inside for hours on end.
   NOUN   VERB

- Break up into _____ teams and have a snowball fight with your
               ADJECTIVE

neighborhood _____.
               PLURAL NOUN

- Sleep the _____ away.
               NOUN

MAD LIBS® is fun to play with friends, but you can also play it by yourself! To begin with, DO NOT look at the story on the page below. Fill in the blanks on this page with the words called for. Then, using the words you have selected, fill in the blank spaces in the story.

Now you've created your own hilarious MAD LIBS® game!

THE NUTCRACKER

ADJECTIVE _____

NOUN _____

NOUN _____

ADJECTIVE _____

ADJECTIVE _____

NOUN _____

ADJECTIVE _____

PLURAL NOUN _____

ADJECTIVE _____

PLURAL NOUN _____

TYPE OF FOOD _____

TYPE OF LIQUID _____

VERB ENDING IN "ING" _____

ADJECTIVE _____

ADJECTIVE _____

MAD LIBS
THE NUTCRACKER

The Nutcracker is a famous ballet that tells the _____
                                                    ADJECTIVE

story of a little _____ named Clara whose godfather gives
                  NOUN

her a/an _____-cracker for Christmas. Amazingly, the nutcracker
         NOUN

comes to life as a/an _____ prince who rescues Clara from some
                      ADJECTIVE

very _____ mice. Then Clara and her prince travel to a magical
     ADJECTIVE

_____, where they are greeted by _____ snowflakes
  NOUN   ADJECTIVE

and dancing _____. They continue their enchanted journey and
            PLURAL NOUN

enter the _____ land of the Sugar Plum _____, where
          ADJECTIVE   PLURAL NOUN

people dressed like _____ and _____ dance for
                    TYPE OF FOOD   TYPE OF LIQUID

them. When the festivities are over, Clara finds herself at home,

_____ under the Christmas tree and holding her _____
VERB ENDING IN "ING"   ADJECTIVE

nutcracker. It was all just a/an _____ dream!
                                 ADJECTIVE

SANTA TALKS

NOUN _____

ADJECTIVE _____

NOUN _____

NOUN _____

NOUN _____

PLURAL NOUN _____

NUMBER _____

PLURAL NOUN _____

PART OF THE BODY _____

NOUN _____

ADJECTIVE _____

PLURAL NOUN _____

ADJECTIVE _____

ADJECTIVE _____

ADJECTIVE _____

MAD LIBS® is fun to play with friends, but you can also play it by yourself! To begin with, DO NOT look at the story on the page below. Fill in the blanks on this page with the words called for. Then, using the words you have selected, fill in the blank spaces in the story.

Now you've created your own hilarious MAD LIBS® game!

MAD LIBS
SANTA TALKS

The following is an exclusive interview at the North _____ with
_____NOUN

the rotund man in the _____ suit:
_____ADJECTIVE

Q: You are described as a jolly _____. Are you that way 24/7?
_____NOUN

A: Ho, ho, ho. Does that answer your _____?
_____NOUN

Q: My next _____ may be somewhat embarrassing. Have you put
_____NOUN

on some extra _____ recently?
_____PLURAL NOUN

A: I'm actually at my average weight of _____ pounds.
_____NUMBER

Q: Doesn't that make it difficult for you to get down chimneys, especially

carrying a sack full of children's _____?
_____PLURAL NOUN

A: No, I just suck in my _____ and squeeze down the
_____PART OF THE BODY

_____. I'm sorry, we're going to have to cut this _____
NOUN _____ADJECTIVE

interview short. I've got to get all the kids' _____ delivered.
_____PLURAL NOUN

Q: Wait—how do you get around the _____ world in one night?
_____ADJECTIVE

A: I have a/an _____ sleigh and a/an _____
_____ADJECTIVE _____ADJECTIVE

team of reindeer—and remember, most of the world is downhill

these days. Ho, ho, ho!

MAD LIBS® is fun to play with friends, but you can also play it by yourself! To begin with, DO NOT look at the story on the page below. Fill in the blanks on this page with the words called for. Then, using the words you have selected, fill in the blank spaces in the story.

Now you've created your own hilarious MAD LIBS® game!

CHRISTMAS COOKIES

NOUN _____

NOUN _____

PLURAL NOUN _____

PLURAL NOUN _____

PLURAL NOUN _____

PLURAL NOUN _____

PLURAL NOUN _____

PLURAL NOUN _____

NOUN _____

PLURAL NOUN _____

NOUN _____

ADJECTIVE _____

ADJECTIVE _____

ADVERB _____

ADJECTIVE _____

ADJECTIVE _____

ADJECTIVE _____

CHRISTMAS COOKIES

Whether red or green, covered with sprinkles or just plain, old

_____, Christmas cookies are the _____'s meow! Some
　　　NOUN　　　　　　　　　　　　　　　　　　　　NOUN

of the tastiest of these _____ include:
　　　　　　　　　　PLURAL NOUN

• Sugar _____: These rank as one of the most popular
　　　　　PLURAL NOUN

Christmas _____. They are often shaped like Christmas
　　　　　PLURAL NOUN

_____ and _____, with frosting and _____
　PLURAL NOUN　　　　PLURAL NOUN　　　　　　　　　PLURAL NOUN

sprinkled on top.

• _____ macaroons: These coconut _____ delight
　　NOUN　　　　　　　　　　　　　　　　　　PLURAL NOUN

the _____-buds, especially when they've been dipped in
　　　NOUN

rich and _____ chocolate.
　　　　ADJECTIVE

• Gingerbread cookies: Who can resist the _____ aroma of these
　　　　　　　　　　　　　　　　　　　　ADJECTIVE

_____ baked spicy classics? At Christmastime they are usually
　ADVERB

cut into the shape of _____ girls and _____ boys,
　　　　　　　　　ADJECTIVE　　　　　　　ADJECTIVE

and many families also build _____ gingerbread houses.
　　　　　　　　　　　　ADJECTIVE

MAD LIBS® is fun to play with friends, but you can also play it by yourself! To begin with, DO NOT look at the story on the page below. Fill in the blanks on this page with the words called for. Then, using the words you have selected, fill in the blank spaces in the story.

Now you've created your own hilarious MAD LIBS® game!

HOLIDAY ADVICE COLUMN

_____ PERSON IN ROOM (FEMALE)

_____ ADVERB

_____ PERSON IN ROOM

_____ NOUN

_____ NOUN

_____ ADJECTIVE

_____ NOUN

_____ NOUN

_____ ADVERB

_____ ADJECTIVE

_____ A PLACE

_____ SAME ADJECTIVE

_____ ADJECTIVE

_____ A PLACE

_____ PART OF THE BODY

_____ NOUN

_____ A PLACE

_____ ADJECTIVE

MAD LIBS

HOLIDAY ADVICE COLUMN

Dear Miss _____,
              PERSON IN ROOM (FEMALE)

I _____ need your advice. I have to buy a Christmas present for
    ADVERB

my friend, _____. We've known each other since the first day of
         PERSON IN ROOM

_____ school, and he/she means the _____ to me. So
  NOUN   NOUN

here's my _____ problem—my friend already owns every
      ADJECTIVE

_____ known to man. What do I get for the _____ who
  NOUN   NOUN

has everything?

_____ yours, _____ in (the) _____.
   ADVERB   ADJECTIVE   A PLACE

Dear _____,
     SAME ADJECTIVE

The solution to your _____ dilemma is easy! We're talking about
            ADJECTIVE

your best friend in all of (the) _____. It doesn't matter
                        A PLACE

what you give—so long as it comes from the _____. Try
                                PART OF THE BODY

making your friend a homemade _____, or give him/her a gift
                      NOUN

certificate to (the) _____. No matter what you decide, your
             A PLACE

friend will appreciate the _____ thought.
                 ADJECTIVE

A SPECIAL RECIPE FOR HOT CHOCOLATE

_____ ADJECTIVE

_____ PART OF THE BODY (PLURAL)

_____ PLURAL NOUN

_____ ADJECTIVE

_____ TYPE OF LIQUID

_____ NOUN

_____ NOUN

_____ ADJECTIVE

_____ NUMBER

_____ NUMBER

_____ ADVERB

_____ ADJECTIVE

_____ NOUN

_____ NOUN

_____ ADJECTIVE

_____ NOUN

MAD LIBS
A SPECIAL RECIPE FOR HOT CHOCOLATE

There is nothing more comforting than a/an _____, frothy hot
ADJECTIVE

chocolate to warm up your _____ on the coldest
PART OF THE BODY (PLURAL)

_____ of winter. Here is a recipe that has been passed down from
PLURAL NOUN

generation to generation in my _____ family. Pour one cup of
ADJECTIVE

_____, one _____ of half-and-half, one tablespoon of
TYPE OF LIQUID   NOUN

vanilla, and two ounces of semisweet _____ into a/an _____
NOUN   ADJECTIVE

pan. Place it on the stove and heat at _____ degrees for
NUMBER

_____ minutes. Stir _____ until the chocolate melts.
NUMBER   ADVERB

Pour the liquid into two _____ mugs and serve with a dollop of
ADJECTIVE

whipped _____ on top. If you add some atmosphere, your
NOUN

_____ will taste even better: Enjoy your drink in front of a/an
NOUN

_____ fireplace or while watching the _____-flakes fall
ADJECTIVE   NOUN

outside your window.

HOW TO MAKE A SNOWMAN

ADJECTIVE _____

PLURAL NOUN _____

ADJECTIVE _____

ADJECTIVE _____

PART OF THE BODY _____

NOUN _____

ADJECTIVE _____

PLURAL NOUN _____

PART OF THE BODY (PLURAL) _____

NOUN _____

PART OF THE BODY _____

NOUN _____

NOUN _____

PLURAL NOUN _____

NOUN _____

ADJECTIVE _____

NOUN _____

Want to make a/an _____ snowman? All you need is some snow
<small>ADJECTIVE</small>

and a few household _____. Then just follow this
<small>PLURAL NOUN</small>

_____ step-by-step guide:
<small>ADJECTIVE</small>

• Roll three _____ balls out of snow: one for the base, one
<small>ADJECTIVE</small>

for the torso, and one for the _____. Then pile them on
<small>PART OF THE BODY</small>

top of one another so they resemble a/an _____.
<small>NOUN</small>

• To complete your snowman's _____ body, use some long,
<small>ADJECTIVE</small>

thin _____ for arms and give him a pair of
<small>PLURAL NOUN</small>

_____ made of coal. Then add a button _____
<small>PART OF THE BODY (PLURAL)</small>   <small>NOUN</small>

and a carrot _____.
<small>PART OF THE BODY</small>

• You can accessorize your snowy creation with a corncob _____,
<small>NOUN</small>

a stovepipe _____, and some buttons made of _____.
<small>NOUN</small>   <small>PLURAL NOUN</small>

If it's really cold outside, you can give him a knitted _____.
<small>NOUN</small>

• And don't forget to give your snowman a name! _____
<small>ADJECTIVE</small>

the _____-man is always a popular choice.
<small>NOUN</small>

MAD LIBS® is fun to play with friends, but you can also play it by yourself! To begin with, DO NOT look at the story on the page below. Fill in the blanks on this page with the words called for. Then, using the words you have selected, fill in the blank spaces in the story.

Now you've created your own hilarious MAD LIBS® game!

ELF-MAIL

_____ PERSON IN ROOM

_____ PERSON IN ROOM

_____ ADJECTIVE

_____ ADJECTIVE

_____ ADJECTIVE

_____ PLURAL NOUN

_____ ADJECTIVE

_____ PERSON IN ROOM

_____ NOUN

_____ ADJECTIVE

_____ ADJECTIVE

_____ PERSON IN ROOM

_____ NOUN

_____ VERB

_____ PLURAL NOUN

MAD LIBS

ELF-MAIL

To: _____-elf@santasworkshop.elf

PERSON IN ROOM

From: _____ slittlehelper@santasworkshop.elf

PERSON IN ROOM

Hi there, _____ buddy! Just wanted to drop you a/an

ADJECTIVE

_____ note to see how you are doing. It's been a/an

ADJECTIVE

_____ Christmas season here. I've made so many toys—

ADJECTIVE

especially jack-in-the-_____—that I've lost count! On another

PLURAL NOUN

_____ note, are you getting excited about _____'s

ADJECTIVE   PERSON IN ROOM

Christmas Eve elf party? I hear DJ _____ Elf will be spinning some

NOUN

really _____ Christmas tunes! I've also got some

ADJECTIVE

_____ gossip: I hear _____ is a shoo-in for Elf of

ADJECTIVE   PERSON IN ROOM

the Year! He/She totally deserves it for being such a hardworking

_____. Well, I've gotta _____—it's back to the

NOUN   VERB

_____ at the workshop. See you soon!

PLURAL NOUN

MAD LIBS® is fun to play with friends, but you can also play it by yourself! To begin with, DO NOT look at the story on the page below. Fill in the blanks on this page with the words called for. Then, using the words you have selected, fill in the blank spaces in the story.

Now you've created your own hilarious MAD LIBS® game!

A CHRISTMAS CARD

_____ ADJECTIVE

_____ ADJECTIVE

_____ NOUN

_____ NOUN

_____ ADJECTIVE

_____ PLURAL NOUN

_____ PLURAL NOUN

_____ ADJECTIVE

_____ NOUN

_____ ADJECTIVE

_____ VERB

_____ ADJECTIVE

_____ NOUN

_____ PLURAL NOUN

_____ NOUN

_____ NOUN

_____ PERSON IN ROOM

MAD LIBS
A CHRISTMAS CARD

Dear Grandma and Grandpa,

Merry Christmas to my wonderful, _____ grandparents. Our
ADJECTIVE

house is filled with _____ Christmas spirit. Yesterday, we went to
ADJECTIVE

the _____ farm and bought a ten-foot-tall _____. We
NOUN   NOUN

put it in our _____ living room and covered it with lights and
ADJECTIVE

_____. Dad decorated the front of the house with strings of
PLURAL NOUN

_____ and _____ decorations. And Mom baked a lot
PLURAL NOUN   ADJECTIVE

of _____ cookies that smell absolutely _____! I hope
NOUN   ADJECTIVE

you're excited about coming to _____ with us! I can't wait to see
VERB

you at our _____ Christmas dinner. We're having your
ADJECTIVE

favorite—roast _____ and mashed _____! And, of
NOUN   PLURAL NOUN

course, _____ pie for dessert!
NOUN

Love from your grand-_____,
NOUN

_____
PERSON IN ROOM

MAD LIBS®

WINTER GAMES
MAD LIBS

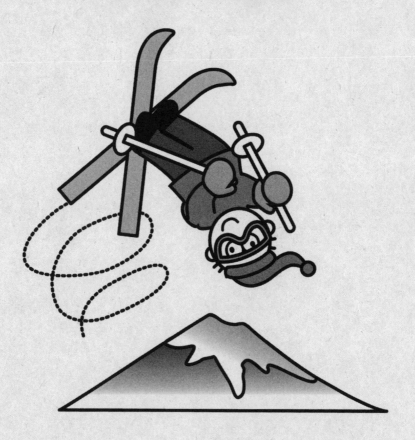

by Roger Price and Leonard Stern

MAD  LIBS

INSTRUCTIONS

MAD LIBS® is a game for people who don't like games!
It can be played by one, two, three, four, or forty.

• RIDICULOUSLY SIMPLE DIRECTIONS

In this tablet you will find stories containing blank spaces where words are left out. One player, the READER, selects one of these stories. The READER does not tell anyone what the story is about. Instead, he/she asks the other players, the WRITERS, to give him/her words. These words are used to fill in the blank spaces in the story.

• TO PLAY

The READER asks each WRITER in turn to call out a word—an adjective or a noun or whatever the space calls for—and uses them to fill in the blank spaces in the story. The result is a MAD LIBS® game.

When the READER then reads the completed MAD LIBS® game to the other players, they will discover that they have written a story that is fantastic, screamingly funny, shocking, silly, crazy, or just plain dumb—depending upon which words each WRITER called out.

• EXAMPLE (*Before* and *After*)

"_____!" he said _____
    EXCLAMATION   ADVERB

as he jumped into his convertible _____ and
                                    NOUN

drove off with his _____ wife.
             ADJECTIVE

"*Ouch*!" he said *stupidly*
    EXCLAMATION   ADVERB

as he jumped into his convertible *cat* and
                                      NOUN

drove off with his *brave* wife.
             ADJECTIVE

QUICK REVIEW

In case you have forgotten what adjectives, adverbs, nouns, and verbs are, here is a quick review:

An ADJECTIVE describes something or somebody. *Lumpy, soft, ugly, messy,* and *short* are adjectives.

An ADVERB tells how something is done. It modifies a verb and usually ends in "ly." *Modestly, stupidly, greedily,* and *carefully* are adverbs.

A NOUN is the name of a person, place, or thing. *Sidewalk, umbrella, bridle, bathtub,* and *nose* are nouns.

A VERB is an action word. *Run, pitch, jump,* and *swim* are verbs. Put the verbs in past tense if the directions say PAST TENSE. *Ran, pitched, jumped,* and *swam* are verbs in the past tense.

When we ask for A PLACE, we mean any sort of place: a country or city *(Spain, Cleveland)* or a room *(bathroom, kitchen).*

An EXCLAMATION or SILLY WORD is any sort of funny sound, gasp, grunt, or outcry, like *Wow!, Ouch!, Whomp!, Ick!,* and *Gadzooks!*

When we ask for specific words, like a NUMBER, a COLOR, an ANIMAL, or a PART OF THE BODY, we mean a word that is one of those things, like *seven, blue, horse,* or *head.*

When we ask for a PLURAL, it means more than one. For example, *cat* pluralized is *cats.*

MAD LIBS® is fun to play with friends, but you can also play it by yourself! To begin with, DO NOT look at the story on the page below. Fill in the blanks on this page with the words called for. Then, using the words you have selected, fill in the blank spaces in the story.

Now you've created your own hilarious MAD LIBS® game!

DOWNHILL SKI RACE

PLURAL NOUN _____

VERB _____

NOUN _____

ADJECTIVE _____

VERB ENDING IN "ING" _____

NOUN _____

PLURAL NOUN _____

NOUN _____

PART OF THE BODY _____

PLURAL NOUN _____

ADJECTIVE _____

PLURAL NOUN _____

NOUN _____

NOUN _____

PLURAL NOUN _____

DOWNHILL SKI RACE

From the moment the downhill _____ leave the gates until the
_{PLURAL NOUN}

second they _____ across the finish line, the ski race is a/an
_{VERB}

_____-pounding experience! The skiers must navigate a/an
_{NOUN}

_____ demanding course: from _____ over giant
_{ADJECTIVE} _{VERB ENDING IN "ING"}

mounds of _____, known as "moguls" to maneuvering around
_{NOUN}

plastic _____ planted in the snow to create a more challenging
_{PLURAL NOUN}

_____. If that isn't tough enough, the racers have to combat the
_{NOUN}

elements—the _____-chilling cold, the blinding snow
_{PART OF THE BODY}

_____, and the _____ winds racing up to 100
_{PLURAL NOUN} _{ADJECTIVE}

_____ per hour. Only the results of a downhill _____
_{PLURAL NOUN} _{NOUN}

are predictable. It seems that year after year a the same team wins this

_____. Must be something in their _____!
_{NOUN} _{PLURAL NOUN}

MAD LIBS® is fun to play with friends, but you can also play it by yourself! To begin with, DO NOT look at the story on the page below. Fill in the blanks on this page with the words called for. Then, using the words you have selected, fill in the blank spaces in the story.

Now you've created your own hilarious MAD LIBS® game!

TRAITS OF ATHLETES

_____ ADJECTIVE

_____ PLURAL NOUN

_____ ADJECTIVE

_____ NOUN

_____ NOUN

_____ PLURAL NOUN

_____ ADJECTIVE

_____ PLURAL NOUN

_____ PLURAL NOUN

_____ PLURAL NOUN

_____ NOUN

_____ ADJECTIVE

_____ ADJECTIVE

_____ NOUN

_____ NOUN

_____ PLURAL NOUN

MAD LIBS
TRAITS OF ATHLETES

A/An _____ survey of both men and _____ winter
_____ADJECTIVE_____   _____PLURAL NOUN_____

game athletes reveals some very _____ statistics:
                                      ____ADJECTIVE____

1. 43 percent are ambidextrous. The right _____ always knows
                                               ___NOUN___

what the left _____ is doing.
                 ___NOUN___

2. 93 percent set impossible _____ for themselves and then achieve
                               __PLURAL NOUN__

these _____ goals.
        ___ADJECTIVE___

3. 47 percent count their calories and eat well-balanced _____—
                                                            __PLURAL NOUN__

observing the recommended allowance of fruit and _____.
                                                     __PLURAL NOUN__

4. Slightly over 50 percent play musical _____, the most popular
                                            __PLURAL NOUN__

being the piano, violin, and percussion _____.
                                            ___NOUN___

5. 73 percent have a/an _____ sense of timing and _____
                          ___ADJECTIVE___   ___ADJECTIVE___

eye-to-_____ coordination.
          ___NOUN___

6. 94 percent never drink hard _____ or smoke _____.
                                  ___NOUN___   __PLURAL NOUN__

FIGURE SKATING

PLURAL NOUN _____

ADVERB _____

NAME OF PERSON (FEMALE) _____

NOUN _____

NOUN _____

ADJECTIVE _____

ADJECTIVE _____

ADJECTIVE _____

NOUN _____

VERB _____

ADJECTIVE _____

NOUN _____

NOUN _____

NOUN _____

ADJECTIVE _____

NOUN _____

PLURAL NOUN _____

NOUN _____

MAD LIBS® is fun to play with friends, but you can also play it by yourself! To begin with, DO NOT look at the story on the page below. Fill in the blanks on this page with the words called for. Then, using the words you have selected, fill in the blank spaces in the story.

Now you've created your own hilarious MAD LIBS® game!

MAD LIBS
FIGURE SKATING

As a crowd of more than 19,000 _____ filed into the _____
                                    PLURAL NOUN   ADVERB

designed auditorium, _____, our _____-skating
                        NAME OF PERSON (FEMALE)   NOUN

champion, went through her warm-up _____. For the first time
                                            NOUN

in her _____ life, the champion felt frightened and _____.
          ADJECTIVE   ADJECTIVE

As the music began, the champion took a/an _____ breath,
                                                ADJECTIVE

smoothed the ruffles of her _____, and started to _____.
                               NOUN   VERB

Just as she feared, when it came time for her most _____ jump, a
                                                        ADJECTIVE

triple _____, she lost her balance and landed with a thump on her
          NOUN

_____. She stood up bravely, brushed the ice off her _____,
    NOUN   NOUN

and finished her _____ routine. The crowd gave her a five-
                    ADJECTIVE

minute standing _____. Even though she realized she had lost the
                    NOUN

competition, she knew she had won the hearts and _____ of every
                                                    PLURAL NOUN

_____ in the auditorium.
    NOUN

RULES FOR A SNOWBALL FIGHT

_____ ADJECTIVE

_____ VERB ENDING IN "ING"

_____ NOUN

_____ PLURAL NOUN

_____ PLURAL NOUN

_____ NOUN

_____ PLURAL NOUN

_____ PART OF THE BODY

_____ NOUN

_____ PLURAL NOUN

_____ PLURAL NOUN

_____ ADVERB

_____ ADJECTIVE

_____ NOUN

_____ PLURAL NOUN

_____ ADJECTIVE

_____ NOUN

_____ NOUN

The _____ winter games committee does not recognize snowball
      ADJECTIVE

_____ as an official _____. Nevertheless, it has
VERB ENDING IN "ING"   NOUN

established rules and _____ for the athletes who want to throw icy
              PLURAL NOUN

_____ at each other.
PLURAL NOUN

- Contestants can toss only one _____ at a time and
                           NOUN

  from a distance not less than 25 _____ away.
                      PLURAL NOUN

- Aiming at a/an _____ is not permitted. If anybody is
              PART OF THE BODY

  hit below the _____, that person automatically wins.
            NOUN

- Loading a snowball with heavy _____ or solid
                       PLURAL NOUN

  _____ is _____ forbidden. Snowball
  PLURAL NOUN   ADVERB

  tampering will result in _____ penalties or rejection
                    ADJECTIVE

  from the _____.
       NOUN

- All _____ must wear _____ gear that protects
    PLURAL NOUN   ADJECTIVE

  their eyes, as well as their _____ and _____.
               NOUN   NOUN

A WINTER GAMES BROADCAST

CELEBRITY (MALE) _____

NOUN _____

NOUN _____

PLURAL NOUN _____

PLURAL NOUN _____

PERSON IN ROOM (MALE) _____

NOUN _____

NOUN _____

PLURAL NOUN _____

NOUN _____

PLURAL NOUN _____

NOUN _____

ADVERB _____

NOUN _____

PLURAL NOUN _____

SAME PERSON IN ROOM (MALE) _____

ADJECTIVE _____

MAD LIBS

A WINTER GAMES BROADCAST

"Hi, we're broadcasting live from the American compound here at the ski

village. Unfortunately, my co-host, _____, has laryngitis and has
                                      CELEBRITY (MALE)

lost his _____. He'll be back with us as soon as his _____
          NOUN   NOUN

returns. Now to breaking _____! Sadly, we've learned that less than
                          PLURAL NOUN

twenty _____ ago, _____, America's best
        PLURAL NOUN   PERSON IN ROOM (MALE)

_____ skier and favorite to win the giant slalom, suffered a life
    NOUN

threatening _____ when he plummeted 300 _____
                NOUN   PLURAL NOUN

down the side of a/an _____. According to the latest hospital
                          NOUN

_____, he broke his _____, but doctors are hopeful he'll
  PLURAL NOUN   NOUN

heal _____ and be back on his _____ by the end of the
          ADVERB   NOUN

year. Our fervent _____ go out to _____ and
                     PLURAL NOUN   SAME PERSON IN ROOM (MALE)

his entire _____ family."
                ADJECTIVE

MAD LIBS® is fun to play with friends, but you can also play it by yourself! To begin with, DO NOT look at the story on the page below. Fill in the blanks on this page with the words called for. Then, using the words you have selected, fill in the blank spaces in the story.

Now you've created your own hilarious MAD LIBS® game!

SNOWBOARDING

_____
PLURAL NOUN

_____
NOUN

_____
PLURAL NOUN

_____
PLURAL NOUN

_____
PLURAL NOUN

_____
ADJECTIVE

_____
ADJECTIVE

_____
NOUN

_____
PART OF THE BODY

_____
NOUN

_____
PLURAL NOUN

_____
VERB

_____
NOUN

_____
NOUN

_____
PLURAL NOUN

_____
ADJECTIVE

_____
VERB ENDING IN "ING"

_____
PLURAL NOUN

MAD LIBS
SNOWBOARDING

Most of us have watched snowboarding spring up before our very

_____. In its short history, _____-boarding has
     PLURAL NOUN   NOUN

cemented itself into the _____ of sporting _____ around
                              PLURAL NOUN   PLURAL NOUN

the world. Its simplicity appeals to men and _____ of all ages. All
                                                  PLURAL NOUN

you need to snowboard is a/an _____ boot, a relatively short
                                    ADJECTIVE

_____ board, athletic _____, and a willingness to
     ADJECTIVE   NOUN

break a/an _____. I am a high-school _____ who
              PART OF THE BODY   NOUN

has won several _____ in snowboarding competitions. Many of my
                    PLURAL NOUN

closest friends say I eat, drink, and _____ snow-boarding. I
                                          VERB

admit to practicing morning, noon, and _____ but it paid off
                                            NOUN

last week when I was invited to qualify for the team in the freestyle

_____. This is where I can shine. I'm the best at inverted
     NOUN

_____, which are _____ because you're upside down
     PLURAL NOUN   ADJECTIVE

while _____. Excuse me, I'm going now. I can't wait to hit
         VERB ENDING IN "ING"

the fresh _____ out on the slopes!
              PLURAL NOUN

MAD LIBS® is fun to play with friends, but you can also play it by yourself! To begin with, DO NOT look at the story on the page below. Fill in the blanks on this page with the words called for. Then, using the words you have selected, fill in the blank spaces in the story.

Now you've created your own hilarious MAD LIBS® game!

BOBSLEDDING GLOSSARY

_____ PLURAL NOUN

_____ ADJECTIVE

_____ ADJECTIVE

_____ NOUN

_____ PLURAL NOUN

_____ NOUN

_____ NOUN

_____ NOUN

_____ NOUN

_____ PLURAL NOUN

_____ PLURAL NOUN

_____ NOUN

_____ VERB ENDING IN "ING"

_____ ADJECTIVE

_____ VERB

_____ NOUN

_____ PLURAL NOUN

_____ NOUN

MAD LIBS
BOBSLEDDING GLOSSARY

The name "bobsledding" comes from the early racers bobbing their

_____ back and forth to gain the most _____ speed.
   PLURAL NOUN   ADJECTIVE

Here are some _____ phrases to provide a better understanding
                   ADJECTIVE

of this high-speed _____.
                        NOUN

Bobsled: a large sled made up of two _____ linked together. There
                                            PLURAL NOUN

are two sizes, a two-person _____ and a four-_____ sled.
                                NOUN   NOUN

Brakeman: the last _____ to leap onto the _____.
                            NOUN   NOUN

He/she applies the _____ to bring it to a stop. The brakeman must
                       PLURAL NOUN

have very strong _____.
                     PLURAL NOUN

Driver: the front _____ in the bobsled is responsible for
                           NOUN

_____. The driver's _____ goal is to maintain
VERB ENDING IN "ING"   ADJECTIVE

the straightest path down the track.

Pushtime: the amount of time required to _____ a/an
                                                  VERB

_____ over the first 50 _____ of a run.
    NOUN   PLURAL NOUN

WH: abbreviation for "what happened?" Usually said when the

_____ crashes!
    NOUN

SNOWMAN-BUILDING

_____ ADJECTIVE

_____ NOUN

_____ NOUN

_____ ADJECTIVE

_____ NOUN

_____ ADJECTIVE

_____ PLURAL NOUN

_____ PART OF THE BODY (PLURAL)

_____ NOUN

_____ COLOR

_____ NOUN

_____ PLURAL NOUN

_____ ADJECTIVE

_____ NOUN

_____ NOUN

_____ ADJECTIVE

_____ NOUN

_____ NOUN

MAD LIBS® is fun to play with friends, but you can also play it by yourself! To begin with, DO NOT look at the story on the page below. Fill in the blanks on this page with the words called for. Then, using the words you have selected, fill in the blank spaces in the story.

Now you've created your own hilarious MAD LIBS® game!

MAD LIBS
SNOWMAN-BUILDING

Question: What kid hasn't loved the _____ thrill of building

ADJECTIVE

a/an _____ man?

NOUN

Answer: Kids who live where the _____ never stops shining.

NOUN

Nevertheless, snowman-building is one of the most _____

ADJECTIVE

competitions at the winter games. Each team is given several hundred

pounds of powdered _____ to mold and shape into what they

NOUN

hope will be the most _____ snowman anyone has ever laid

ADJECTIVE

_____ on. This year's winner was so adorable that everyone wanted

PLURAL NOUN

to throw their _____ around him and hug his

PART OF THE BODY (PLURAL)

_____. They used a bright _____ _____ for

NOUN · COLOR · NOUN

his nose, two shiny _____ for his eyes and a/an _____

PLURAL NOUN · ADJECTIVE

_____ on his head for a hat. In addition, they put a corncob

NOUN

_____ in his mouth and tied a/an _____ scarf around

NOUN · ADJECTIVE

his neck. Their prizewinning _____ quickly became the talk of the

NOUN

_____.

NOUN

FACE-OFF

_____ NOUN

_____ NOUN

_____ ADJECTIVE

_____ NOUN

_____ NOUN

_____ NOUN

_____ ADJECTIVE

_____ NOUN

_____ ADJECTIVE

_____ NOUN

_____ NOUN

_____ PLURAL NOUN

_____ ADVERB

_____ PLURAL NOUN

_____ PLURAL NOUN

_____ ADJECTIVE

_____ NOUN

_____ PLURAL NOUN

MAD LIBS® is fun to play with friends, but you can also play it by yourself! To begin with, DO NOT look at the story on the page below. Fill in the blanks on this page with the words called for. Then, using the words you have selected, fill in the blank spaces in the story.

Now you've created your own hilarious MAD LIBS® game!

MAD LIBS
FACE-OFF

If you're seeking fame and _____ as a hockey player, you may want
                                      NOUN

to give it a second _____. Hockey is not a sport for the _____
                          NOUN   ADJECTIVE

of heart! You put your _____ in danger the moment you enter the
                              NOUN

rink and skate onto the _____. Hockey is a game of vicious
                                NOUN

_____ contact. To be a/an _____ hockey player you
      NOUN   ADJECTIVE

have to keep your _____ in perfect shape, you have to be lean and
                          NOUN

_____, and you can't afford one extra ounce of _____
      ADJECTIVE   NOUN

on your _____. Hockey attracts the most volatile _____.
              NOUN   PLURAL NOUN

These fans can become _____ physical and throw soda _____,
                              ADVERB   PLURAL NOUN

large sticks and _____, and even _____ coins onto the
                    PLURAL NOUN   ADJECTIVE

ice. You can see why hockey is considered the most physical _____
                                                                    NOUN

of all the _____ at the winter games.
              PLURAL NOUN

From WINTER GAMES MAD LIBS® • Copyright © 2005 by Penguin Random House LLC.

DOGS AND SLEDS

_____ PLURAL NOUN

_____ PLURAL NOUN

_____ NOUN

_____ PART OF THE BODY

_____ ADVERB

_____ NOUN

_____ NOUN

_____ PLURAL NOUN

_____ PLURAL NOUN

_____ NUMBER

_____ ADJECTIVE

_____ PLURAL NOUN

_____ NOUN

_____ NOUN

_____ PLURAL NOUN

_____ NOUN

_____ NOUN

MAD LIBS

DOGS AND SLEDS

Of all the winter _____, dogsled racing is my favorite. Watching
                  PLURAL NOUN

these beautiful four-legged _____ courageously pull the sled across
                             PLURAL NOUN

the frozen _____ tugs at my _____ strings. The
               NOUN   PART OF THE BODY

rules for dogsled racing are _____ simple—the first team to cross
                            ADVERB

the finish _____ wins the _____. A dogsled team consists
             NOUN   NOUN

of 14 Siberian _____, each weighing approximately 50 _____
             PLURAL NOUN   PLURAL NOUN

and each able to pull _____ times its weight. These beautiful and
                  NUMBER

_____ dogs are trained to respond to the shouted _____
    ADJECTIVE   PLURAL NOUN

of their _____. The driver stands on a/an _____ at the
          NOUN   NOUN

rear of the sled and guides the dogs with verbal _____ and, if
                                 PLURAL NOUN

necessary, a crack of his _____. Dogsled races are proof positive
                     NOUN

why a dog is thought of as man's best _____.
                                NOUN

MAD LIBS® is fun to play with friends, but you can also play it by yourself! To begin with, DO NOT look at the story on the page below. Fill in the blanks on this page with the words called for. Then, using the words you have selected, fill in the blank spaces in the story.

Now you've created your own hilarious MAD LIBS® game!

THE LODGE

_____
NOUN

_____
NOUN

_____
NOUN

_____
NOUN

_____
PLURAL NOUN

_____
NOUN

_____
ADJECTIVE

_____
NOUN

_____
NOUN

_____
VERB ENDING IN "ING"

_____
PART OF THE BODY

_____
NOUN

_____
NOUN

_____
PLURAL NOUN

_____
PLURAL NOUN

_____
NOUN

_____
ADJECTIVE

_____
PLURAL NOUN

MAD LIBS®
THE LODGE

A/An _____ away from home is most important to a competitive
<u>NOUN</u>

_____. Athletes should select a lodge recommended by a travel
<u>NOUN</u>

_____, the automobile _____, even relatives or close
<u>NOUN</u>   <u>NOUN</u>

_____. The bedroom should have a king-size _____ with
<u>PLURAL NOUN</u>   <u>NOUN</u>

a/an _____ mattress to ensure a good night's _____. If
<u>ADJECTIVE</u>   <u>NOUN</u>

possible, there should be a hot _____ to relax those aching muscles
<u>NOUN</u>

after a long day of _____. Since relaxation is so important to
<u>VERB ENDING IN "ING"</u>

an athlete's _____, the lodge should also provide an outdoor
<u>PART OF THE BODY</u>

swimming _____. Other amenities might be a wood-burning
<u>NOUN</u>

_____, a game room stocked with arcade _____, game
<u>NOUN</u>   <u>PLURAL NOUN</u>

tables for chess or _____, as well as a Ping-Pong _____.
<u>PLURAL NOUN</u>   <u>NOUN</u>

Since nutrition is of _____ significance to athletes, the lodge's
<u>ADJECTIVE</u>

restaurant should have a rating of five _____.
<u>PLURAL NOUN</u>

MAD LIBS® is fun to play with friends, but you can also play it by yourself! To begin with, DO NOT look at the story on the page below. Fill in the blanks on this page with the words called for. Then, using the words you have selected, fill in the blank spaces in the story.

Now you've created your own hilarious MAD LIBS® game!

SAGE ADVICE

VERB ENDING IN "ING" _____

NAME OF PERSON IN ROOM _____

ADJECTIVE _____

ADJECTIVE _____

PLURAL NOUN _____

ADVERB _____

PLURAL NOUN _____

ADJECTIVE _____

PLURAL NOUN _____

NOUN _____

ADJECTIVE _____

PLURAL NOUN _____

PLURAL NOUN _____

VERB ENDING IN "ING" _____

NOUN _____

MAD LIBS

SAGE ADVICE

According to the pioneer of downhill _____, _____,
VERB ENDING IN "ING" NAME OF PERSON IN ROOM

"When you ski, your _____ equipment should be the equal of your
ADJECTIVE

_____ ability." Remember this sage advice when purchasing your
ADJECTIVE

first pair of _____. It is _____ important to take many
PLURAL NOUN ADVERB

_____ into consideration before plunking down _____
PLURAL NOUN ADJECTIVE

bucks for your _____. Your gender, your height, and your
PLURAL NOUN

_____ are all _____ factors in selecting a pair of
NOUN ADJECTIVE

_____ that match your skills and _____. It goes
PLURAL NOUN PLURAL NOUN

without _____: If you don't have the right skis, you're starting
VERB ENDING IN "ING"

off on the wrong _____.
NOUN

MORE SAGE ADVICE

NOUN _____

NOUN _____

PLURAL NOUN _____

ADVERB _____

ADJECTIVE _____

PART OF THE BODY _____

NOUN _____

ADJECTIVE _____

NOUN _____

ADJECTIVE _____

NOUN _____

PART OF THE BODY _____

ADJECTIVE _____

NOUN _____

NOUN _____

ADJECTIVE _____

NOUN _____

NOUN _____

MAD LIBS® is fun to play with friends, but you can also play it by yourself! To begin with, DO NOT look at the story on the page below. Fill in the blanks on this page with the words called for. Then, using the words you have selected, fill in the blank spaces in the story.

Now you've created your own hilarious MAD LIBS® game!

MORE SAGE ADVICE

Beware! If your skiing equipment isn't top-of-the-_____, you put
NOUN

your _____ at risk. Here are some important _____ to
NOUN   PLURAL NOUN

remember:

Ski Boots: Give careful thought to this important piece of equipment.

Choose _____. Together with ski bindings, these _____
ADVERB   ADJECTIVE

boots form the link between your skis and your _____.
PART OF THE BODY

Ski Bindings: As far as your safety is concerned, _____ bindings
NOUN

are the most _____ pieces of _____ in skiing. If you
ADJECTIVE   NOUN

have any _____ questions, seek the help of a/an _____
ADJECTIVE   NOUN

professional.

Ski Helmets: Protect your _____ by wearing a/an
PART OF THE BODY

_____ ski _____. Helmets absolutely help you avoid a
ADJECTIVE   NOUN

serious _____ mishap.
NOUN

Ski Clothing: First and foremost, get yourself some _____
ADJECTIVE

underwear, preferably thermal, to keep your _____ warm. You will
NOUN

also need a ski _____ to protect your head and ears from extremely
NOUN

frigid temperatures.

SLED RACE

NOUN _____

NOUN _____

NOUN _____

PLURAL NOUN _____

NOUN _____

PLURAL NOUN _____

PLURAL NOUN _____

NOUN _____

ADJECTIVE _____

PLURAL NOUN _____

ADJECTIVE _____

NOUN _____

ADJECTIVE _____

NOUN _____

PLURAL NOUN _____

PART OF THE BODY _____

ADJECTIVE _____

PLURAL NOUN _____

MAD LIBS® is fun to play with friends, but you can also play it by yourself! To begin with, DO NOT look at the story on the page below. Fill in the blanks on this page with the words called for. Then, using the words you have selected, fill in the blank spaces in the story.

Now you've created your own hilarious MAD LIBS® game!

MAD LIBS
SLED RACE

Ever since I was in the fifth _____ in school I've dreamed of having
                                      NOUN

my own sled. I started delivering the morning _____ on my two-
                                                        NOUN

wheeler _____ until I saved enough pennies, nickels, and
            NOUN

_____ to buy one. It was the smartest _____
    PLURAL NOUN   NOUN

I ever made. Today, I am a champion sled racer with nine first-place

_____, seven second-place _____, one third-place
    PLURAL NOUN   PLURAL NOUN

_____, and four _____ ribbons. Although some of my
    NOUN   ADJECTIVE

competitors use sophisticated and aerodynamic _____, I still rely
                                                      PLURAL NOUN

on a/an _____ version of my old sledding _____. Sled
            ADJECTIVE   NOUN

racing is relatively simple; the participants line up at the top of a/an

_____ hill. When the starter drops his _____,
    ADJECTIVE   NOUN

the competitors climb on their _____ and race at break
                                      PLURAL NOUN

_____ speed to cross the _____ line ahead of the
  PART OF THE BODY   ADJECTIVE

other _____.
          PLURAL NOUN

MAD LIBS® is fun to play with friends, but you can also play it by yourself! To begin with, DO NOT look at the story on the page below. Fill in the blanks on this page with the words called for. Then, using the words you have selected, fill in the blank spaces in the story.

Now you've created your own hilarious MAD LIBS® game!

SKI JUMPING

_____ NOUN

_____ NOUN

_____ ADJECTIVE

_____ NOUN

_____ PLURAL NOUN

_____ NOUN

_____ ADVERB

_____ NOUN

_____ ADJECTIVE

_____ NOUN

_____ NOUN

_____ PLURAL NOUN

_____ PART OF THE BODY

_____ NOUN

_____ PART OF THE BODY

_____ VERB ENDING IN "ING"

_____ PLURAL NOUN

_____ PLURAL NOUN

MAD LIBS

SKI JUMPING

Whether you're a/an _____ seated in the stands or a/an
NOUN

_____ watching on television, the _____ beauty of ski
NOUN   ADJECTIVE

jumping is dramatically apparent. What compares to a skier taking flight,

soaring into the crystal-clear _____, against a background of blue
NOUN

_____ with _____-capped mountains looming
PLURAL NOUN   NOUN

_____ in the distance? But _____ jumping doesn't
ADVERB   NOUN

shortchange you on thrills. There's _____ drama in every jump.
ADJECTIVE

You can't help but sit on the edge of your _____ and hold your
NOUN

_____ as conflicting _____ race through your
NOUN   PLURAL NOUN

_____. Will the skier break the world _____? Will
PART OF THE BODY   NOUN

he or she break a/an _____? Minutes later, the crowd is
PART OF THE BODY

_____ at the top of their _____ and you have your
VERB ENDING IN "ING"   PLURAL NOUN

answer. You've got a world champion on your _____.
PLURAL NOUN

SPEED SKATING

NOUN _____

ADVERB _____

NOUN _____

PLURAL NOUN _____

PART OF THE BODY (PLURAL) _____

NOUN _____

VERB ENDING IN "ING" _____

NOUN _____

NOUN _____

PLURAL NOUN _____

PLURAL NOUN _____

ADVERB _____

NOUN _____

PART OF THE BODY _____

COLOR _____

MAD LIBS® is fun to play with friends, but you can also play it by yourself! To begin with, DO NOT look at the story on the page below. Fill in the blanks on this page with the words called for. Then, using the words you have selected, fill in the blank spaces in the story.

Now you've created your own hilarious MAD LIBS® game!

A speed-skating _____ goes by so _____ that if you
              NOUN   ADVERB

blink a/an _____, you might miss the race. In every competition,
              NOUN

skaters not only race against their fellow _____, they also challenge
                                              PLURAL NOUN

the _____ of the clock. They know a fraction of a/an
        PART OF THE BODY (PLURAL)

_____ can be the difference between not only winning but
      NOUN

_____ a record. Consequently, skaters worship at the shrine
   VERB ENDING IN "ING"

of speed. When racing, they skate bent over, angled toward the ice, with one

_____ behind them, pressed firmly against their _____,
      NOUN   NOUN

to eliminate being slowed down by wind resistance. They even wear skintight

_____ to improve their speed. And, as you can tell from their trim,
   PLURAL NOUN

muscular _____, skaters are _____ weight-conscious.
         PLURAL NOUN   ADVERB

An extra ounce of _____ strikes terror in a skater's _____.
               NOUN   PART OF THE BODY

To say speed skaters are neurotic is like calling a kettle _____!
                                                   COLOR

MAD LIBS® is fun to play with friends, but you can also play it by yourself! To begin with, DO NOT look at the story on the page below. Fill in the blanks on this page with the words called for. Then, using the words you have selected, fill in the blank spaces in the story.

Now you've created your own hilarious MAD LIBS® game!

THE LUGE

_____ ADJECTIVE

_____ PLURAL NOUN

_____ PLURAL NOUN

_____ NOUN

_____ NOUN

_____ PLURAL NOUN

_____ PLURAL NOUN

_____ NOUN

_____ PART OF THE BODY (PLURAL)

_____ PLURAL NOUN

_____ NOUN

_____ NOUN

_____ PART OF THE BODY (PLURAL)

_____ ADJECTIVE

_____ PLURAL NOUN

_____ ADJECTIVE

_____ NOUN

MAD LIBS
THE LUGE

Although the _____ luge is thought to be relatively new, it's
                    ADJECTIVE

actually one of the oldest of all winter _____. It was a favorite
                                          PLURAL NOUN

activity of kings, queens, and _____ in the eighteenth century. The
                                PLURAL NOUN

word comes from the French _____ for sled. The luge travels at
                            NOUN

a/an _____-threatening speed, often exceeding 75 _____
      NOUN   PLURAL NOUN

per hour. Luge athletes become virtual flying _____ from
                                              PLURAL NOUN

the moment they step into the _____, lie flat on their
                              NOUN

_____, and, with their _____ looking up
PART OF THE BODY (PLURAL)   PLURAL NOUN

into the sky, push off. As they fly down the ice-covered _____,
                                                          NOUN

they steer the _____ by pressing their _____
               NOUN   PART OF THE BODY (PLURAL)

against the front runners. Protected only by a/an _____ helmet,
                                                   ADJECTIVE

they risk their _____ and are in _____ danger until
                PLURAL NOUN   ADJECTIVE

they speed across the finish _____!
                             NOUN

MAD LIBS® is fun to play with friends, but you can also play it by yourself! To begin with, DO NOT look at the story on the page below. Fill in the blanks on this page with the words called for. Then, using the words you have selected, fill in the blank spaces in the story.

Now you've created your own hilarious MAD LIBS® game!

IGLOO-BUILDING CONTEST

ADJECTIVE _____

NOUN _____

PLURAL NOUN _____

ADJECTIVE _____

PLURAL NOUN _____

PLURAL NOUN _____

PLURAL NOUN _____

ADVERB _____

ADJECTIVE _____

PLURAL NOUN _____

NOUN _____

ADVERB _____

NOUN _____

ADJECTIVE _____

ADJECTIVE _____

PLURAL NOUN _____

NOUN _____

ADJECTIVE _____

MAD LIBS
IGLOO-BUILDING CONTEST

Building an igloo is _____ and fun. A hard field of snow is
ADJECTIVE

required to build a/an _____ with a dome. The first rule is to pack
NOUN

the frozen _____ into _____ blocks of all shapes and
PLURAL NOUN   ADJECTIVE

_____. Large _____ are used as the base of the dome and
PLURAL NOUN   PLURAL NOUN

the smaller _____ go on the top. Then, each block should be
PLURAL NOUN

smooth and angled _____ to make a/an _____ bond
ADVERB   ADJECTIVE

with the other _____. Admittedly, building a/an _____
PLURAL NOUN   NOUN

is _____ more difficult than pitching a/an _____, but
ADVERB   NOUN

it keeps the _____ air out better than a tent. A well-built,
ADJECTIVE

average-size igloo can accommodate three adults or five _____
ADJECTIVE

_____. Believe it or not, _____-building contests are
PLURAL NOUN   NOUN

now being held all over—wherever the climate is _____.
ADJECTIVE

MAD LIBS® is fun to play with friends, but you can also play it by yourself! To begin with, DO NOT look at the story on the page below. Fill in the blanks on this page with the words called for. Then, using the words you have selected, fill in the blank spaces in the story.

Now you've created your own hilarious MAD LIBS® game!

SKIING DISCIPLINES

_____ PLURAL NOUN

_____ ADJECTIVE

_____ NOUN

_____ PLURAL NOUN

_____ ADJECTIVE

_____ VERB ENDING IN "ING"

_____ PLURAL NOUN

_____ ADJECTIVE

_____ PLURAL NOUN

_____ PLURAL NOUN

_____ ADJECTIVE

_____ ADJECTIVE

_____ ADJECTIVE

_____ PLURAL NOUN

MAD LIBS
SKIING DISCIPLINES

Skiing comes in different _____, and each has its own
PLURAL NOUN

_____ features offering a different kind of excitement and
ADJECTIVE

_____ for skiers of all _____.
NOUN   PLURAL NOUN

Alpine Skiing: This _____ form of skiing is the most general
ADJECTIVE

_____ discipline and is practiced equally by men and
VERB ENDING IN "ING"

_____.
PLURAL NOUN

Telemark Skiing: This is a/an _____ style of skiing. It uses a
ADJECTIVE

turning technique that is admired by many _____ and mastered by
PLURAL NOUN

few _____.
PLURAL NOUN

Freestyle Skiing: This takes skiing to _____ heights, using skis in
ADJECTIVE

many _____ ways to come up with _____ new
ADJECTIVE   ADJECTIVE

disciplines, jumps, and _____.
PLURAL NOUN

MAD LIBS® is fun to play with friends, but you can also play it by yourself! To begin with, DO NOT look at the story on the page below. Fill in the blanks on this page with the words called for. Then, using the words you have selected, fill in the blank spaces in the story.

Now you've created your own hilarious MAD LIBS® game!

Q & A WITH A
CHAMPION ICE-FISHER

_____ NOUN

_____ NOUN

_____ PLURAL NOUN

_____ PLURAL NOUN

_____ NUMBER

_____ NOUN

_____ NOUN

_____ NOUN

_____ NOUN

_____ ADJECTIVE

_____ PLURAL NOUN

_____ NOUN

_____ PLURAL NOUN

_____ NOUN

_____ PLURAL NOUN

_____ ADJECTIVE

_____ NOUN

Q: How does it feel to win a gold _____?

NOUN

A: I'm bursting with _____. It's as if I've won a million _____.

NOUN   PLURAL NOUN

Q: How do you always know there are _____ under the ice?

PLURAL NOUN

A: You don't. You may have to drill more than _____ holes in the

NUMBER

_____ to catch your first _____.

NOUN   NOUN

Q: What's the most important safety _____ you can give a would-

NOUN

be _____-fisher?

NOUN

A: I always tell them what my _____ grandfather told me: Do

ADJECTIVE

not drill a fishing hole bigger than your waistline!

Q: When you ice-fish, you're battling the _____. How do you

PLURAL NOUN

protect yourself against the _____-chilling cold?

NOUN

A: You have to wear protective _____ or you'll freeze your

PLURAL NOUN

_____. I suggest heavy boots, wool-lined _____, and, of

NOUN   PLURAL NOUN

course, _____-johns are a must.

ADJECTIVE

Q: When is it better to just stay in the comfort of your _____?

NOUN

A: Again, as my grandfather used to say: "If the wind is from the east, fishing

is the least."

MAD LIBS® is fun to play with friends, but you can also play it by yourself! To begin with, DO NOT look at the story on the page below. Fill in the blanks on this page with the words called for. Then, using the words you have selected, fill in the blank spaces in the story.

Now you've created your own hilarious MAD LIBS® game!

AWARD CEREMONIES

_____ ADJECTIVE

_____ NOUN

_____ PLURAL NOUN

_____ PLURAL NOUN

_____ NOUN

_____ PART OF THE BODY

_____ ADJECTIVE

_____ NOUN

_____ ADJECTIVE

_____ PLURAL NOUN

_____ ADJECTIVE

_____ ADJECTIVE

_____ PLURAL NOUN

_____ PLURAL NOUN

MAD LIBS
AWARD CEREMONIES

By far, the most touching and _____ moments of the games are
                                               ADJECTIVE

the _____ ceremonies in which first-, second-, and third-place
    NOUN

_____ are presented to the winning _____. There's
PLURAL NOUN   PLURAL NOUN

hardly a dry _____ in the stadium when the officials shake the
                NOUN

athlete's _____ and place the _____ medal around
       PART OF THE BODY   ADJECTIVE

his/her _____. Perhaps the most memorable and meaningful
      NOUN

moment occurs when the _____ winner is handed a bouquet of
                     ADJECTIVE

_____ and the _____ anthem of his/her country
    PLURAL NOUN   ADJECTIVE

is played. When the song ends, the athletes usually break into

_____ smiles, lift their _____ high in the air, and
   ADJECTIVE   PLURAL NOUN

acknowledge the crowd by waving their _____.
                                PLURAL NOUN

Join the millions of Mad Libs fans creating wacky and wonderful stories on our apps!

Download Mad Libs today!